COWBOY: THE MAN AND THE MYTH

Also by Robin May:

The American West (*with G. A. Embleton*)
Wolfe's Army (*with G. A. Embleton*)
The British Army in the American Revolution 1775-1783 (*with G. A. Embleton*)
The Wild West
The Pleasure of Guns (*with Joseph G. Rosa*)
Gunsmoke: A Study of Violence in the Wild West (*with Joseph G. Rosa: also available from New English Library*)
The Gold Rushes

Also by Joseph G. Rosa:

They Called Him Wild Bill: The Life and Adventures of James Butler Hickok
Alias Jack McCall
The Gunfighter: Man or Myth?
Colonel Colt London

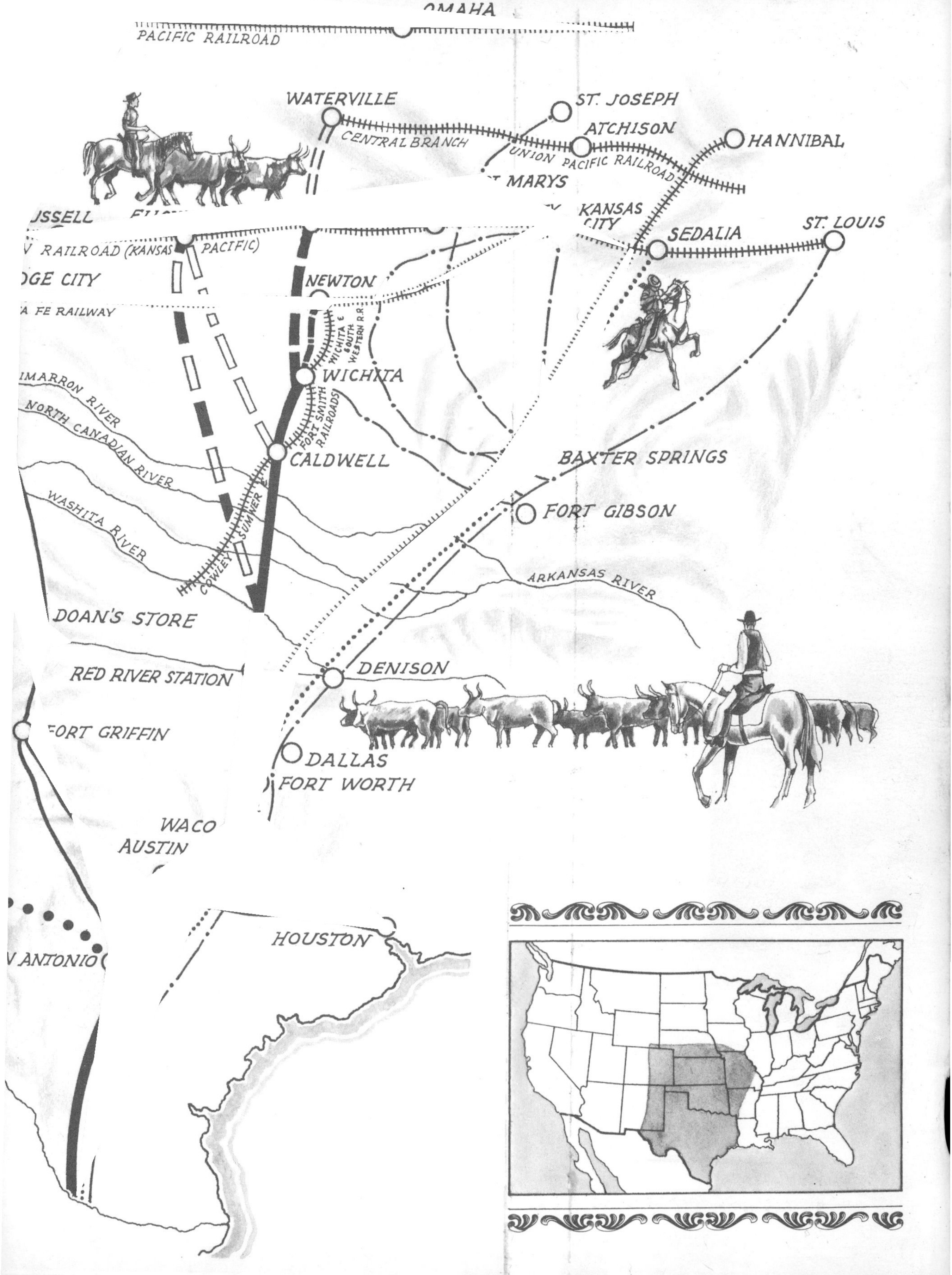
OMAHA
PACIFIC RAILROAD
WATERVILLE
CENTRAL BRANCH
ST. JOSEPH
ATCHISON
UNION PACIFIC RAILROAD
HANNIBAL
MARYS
KANSAS CITY
SEDALIA
ST. LOUIS
USSELL
RAILROAD (KANSAS PACIFIC)
GE CITY
NEWTON
A FE RAILWAY
WICHITA & SOUTH WESTERN R.R.
WICHITA
FORT SMITH RAILROADS
IMARRON RIVER
NORTH CANADIAN RIVER
CALDWELL
BAXTER SPRINGS
WASHITA RIVER
FORT GIBSON
COWLEY SUMNER &
ARKANSAS RIVER
DOAN'S STORE
RED RIVER STATION
DENISON
FORT GRIFFIN
DALLAS
FORT WORTH
WACO
AUSTIN
HOUSTON
N ANTONIO

COWBOY: THE MAN AND THE MYTH

ROBIN MAY and JOSEPH G. ROSA

NEW ENGLISH LIBRARY
TIMES MIRROR

To Wayne Gard of Texas and Everett Dick of Oklahoma, in admiration of their writing on the era of the Longhorns, and to Richard Dillon for the literary trail that we so nearly rode together

First published in Great Britain by New English Library
Barnard's Inn, Holborn, London EC1N 2JR in 1980

Art Editor: Deborah Miles
Design: Mark Holt

Printed in Great Britain by M & A Thomson Litho Ltd,
East Kilbride, Scotland

Bound by Hunter & Foulis, Edinburgh

4500 37819

CONTENTS

1.

INTRODUCTION

A band of 'armed desperadoes known as "Cowboys"' were menaces to the peace of Arizona Territory, so President Chester A. Arthur claimed in his annual message to Congress in December 1881, a statement which is worlds away from Tom Mix, Buck Jones, Roy Rogers and 'Home on the Range'.

The following May, Arthur threatened Arizona with martial law, so alarming were the reports that had been reaching him from Cochise County in general and turbulent Tombstone in particular. For these months were the aftermath of the classic shoot-out at the OK Corral on 26 October 1881, a period of near anarchy, like the months that had preceded it.

So much for the Cowboys of the early 1880s.

It took no less smart a showman than Buffalo Bill Cody to rehabilitate, then popularise, not only the word 'cowboy' but also the breed. In 1884, Cody was to transform a cowpuncher named William Levi Taylor into 'Buck' Taylor, 'The King of the Cowboys', America's first cowboy hero, and, lest patrons of his Wild West show should be nervous of this 6ft 5in 'desperado', publicity men, as Don Russell relates in his classic *The Lives and Legends of Buffalo Bill*, assured audiences that the handsome fellow was 'as amiable as a child'. They were then able to watch him throwing a steer and taming a bucking bronco without sympathising with the animals.

Today, Buck Taylor has lapsed into obscurity, but from him has sprung that most potent of Frontier myths – the romantic hired hand on horseback, the American cowboy. Individual cowboys are now forgotten unless they took the precaution to secure immortality by becoming notorious outlaws. This makes the enduring myth even more remarkable. To those not in love with the Old West to the point of actually studying it, the legendary time and place means Custer, Sitting Bull, Geronimo, Billy the Kid, Wild Bill Hickok, Jesse James, Calamity Jane and a handful of others, not one of them a genuine cowboy. Yet the hired hand stands out as an anonymous, mythical and all-powerful image.

This book is not about the myth as such, yet that myth will never be far from the reader's mind because of its potency and because it will last as long as there are films, television and books to breathe dramatic life into it. (It is an ironic fact that so many

1: William F. 'Buffalo Bill' Cody, circa 1876. Cody is dressed for the part of a scout for his theatrical appearances. Later, in 1883, when his 'Wild West' was launched, his garb, like his show, became even more spectacular.
COURTESY JOSEPH G. ROSA WESTERN AMERICANA COLLECTION.

people call Westerns 'cowboy' films/pictures/movies despite the fact that only a handful are actually about cowboys: some of that handful are considered in Appendix 3).

It must be stressed that this is not a debunking book. Hostility to the cowboy by experts – those who knew him at his considerable worst – will be cited, and much of the evidence of those who can be trusted is searing stuff. Even Joseph G. McCoy, the founding father of the Kansas cowtowns, who had a vested interest in the cowboy, wrote that the 'average cow-boy' in a cowtown would plunge into a 'vortex of dissipation', a 'dance house in full blast', which he characterised thus: 'Few more wild, reckless scenes of abandoned debauchery can be seen on the civilized earth.' And he claimed that the 'cow-boys while drunk ... have brought the *personnel* of the Texan cattle trade into great disrepute'.

Yet by the time the reader of Chapter Two of this book has travelled in imagination with the 'herders' on their long drive to Kansas or beyond, he or she will hardly be surprised that the boys sometimes went wilder than any film to date has dared suggest.

Students of the Old West soon discover the sheer ordinariness of the real cowboy as opposed to his mythical counterpart, that handsome hero on horseback, neither of whose legs is bandy and who is so appealing to the millions who prefer a truly open-air life at a distance. But debunking can go too far. In his masterly introduction to *Cowboy Life*, a series of extracts from notable contemporary accounts of the cattle trade, William Savage states that cowboying required no particular skills beyond the initial ability to sit on a horse and pay attention.

2: An old-style and very early Texas cowboy, from a drawing by Frederic Remington.
COURTESY ROBIN MAY COLLECTION.

Now it would be foolish for cowboy buffs mentally to reach for their six-shooters, because, as Savage notes, 'a multitude of frail and pampered easterners, Britons, Frenchmen, and others learned to ride and rope in shorter order and with equal proficiency'. But the undeniable perils of the long drive – the stampedes, the storms, the river crossings – cannot be underplayed and were often lethal enough to make any fair-minded person admire, as well as thrill to, the exploits of the trail boss and his men. And, too, their sheer endurance was of a sort rarely known except in war. Though even in war, admittedly infinitely more dangerous, combatants get some rest. Not so on the trail. E. C. Abbott, known all over the cowboy's West as Teddy Blue, told Helena Huntington Smith, who collaborated with him in his enthralling *We Pointed them North*, how the loss of sleep was the worst hardship on the trail. A day could end at 9pm, but every man except the boss, the horse wrangler and the cook acted as a night guard for two hours. A cowboy on the trail could snatch about five hours' sleep IF everything was peaceful. If not, he would be lucky to get one hour. The hands sometimes rubbed tobacco juice in their eyes to keep awake and sometimes fell asleep for minutes in the saddle.

And what if the cowboy complained? Said one boss to Teddy Blue: 'What the hell are you kicking about? You can sleep all winter when you get to Montana!'

This must be remembered when set against a typically hostile portrait of the cowboy. Richard Irving Dodge, a soldier who had served with Sherman, was too honest not to mention the good points of a cowboy, but he went on to paint a highly critical picture in his *Our Wild Indians: Thirty-three Years' Personal Experience Among the Red Men of the Great West* (1882):

> For fidelity to duty, for promptness and vigor of action, for resources in difficulty, and unshaken courage in danger, the cow-boy has no superior among men.
>
> But there is something in this peculiar life which develops not only the highest virtues, but the most ignoble of vices. It is not solitude, for the shepherds of the Plains lead lives quite as solitary, and they are generally quiet, inoffensive persons. The cow-boy, on the contrary, is usually the most reckless of all the reckless desperadoes developed on the frontier. Disregarding equally the rights and lives of others, and utterly reckless of his own life; always ready with his weapons and spoiling for a fight, he is the terror of all who come near him, his visits to the frontier towns of Kansas and Nebraska being regarded as a calamity second only to a western tornado. His idea of enjoyment is to fill himself full of bad whiskey, mount his mustang, tear through the streets, whooping, yelling, flourishing and firing his pistols until the streets are deserted and every house closed, then with a grim smile of happiness he dashes off to his comrades to excite their envy by graphic pictures of his own exploits and the terror of the timid townspeople.

3: The Texas cowboy in the mid-1870s, from a drawing by Frederic Remington.
COURTESY ROBIN MAY COLLECTION.

4: By the mid-1880s the cowboy's clothing had achieved an almost 'uniform' appearance. This photograph of C. N. Dunlap, foreman at the Watson Ranch, Kearney, Buffalo County, Nebraska, was made in 1888, and must serve as a graphic example of what a typical hand on the northern range looked like around the time that Buffalo Bill took some cowboys overseas and exhibited them in London during Queen Victoria's Golden Jubilee in 1887.
COURTESY THE SOLOMON D. BUTCHER COLLECTION, NEBRASKA STATE HISTORICAL SOCIETY.

Dodge had another paragraph to rub his message in still more about the 'desperadoes':

> Cattle-stealing is a mania not confined solely to our Scotch ancestors. The frontier has many 'cow-boys' out of employ, many impecunious gentlemen who long yearningly for a herd of cattle. The 'waifs and strays' of large herds, or even a considerable herd, carelessly guarded, will suddenly disappear. Sometimes the herdsmen and the cattle will disappear together . . .

It will already be clear to the reader that there will be no attempt to minimise the notable vices of the cowboy and there will also be no absurd glamorisation of an unglamorous job. But he had many enemies – settlers, northern lawmen, respectable townsmen – who often grossly exaggerated their side of the story. This account of him is not an apology but is written from his point of view.

The now misunderstood and rarely mentioned profession of drover – as opposed to trail boss – will be examined, and, naturally, the cattleman/rancher will get his due: he was the businessman – the capitalist of the range, whose job was to make money, not lose it all in one giant spree, as some of his hands were liable to do. But those hands – and the ones who showed a little more self-control – are the heroes of the myth, and perhaps the reader will find that, as in nearly all the myths of mankind, that of the cowboy has some solid foundation in fact.

Robin May,
Joseph G. Rosa,
London, 1978.

5: Cowboys loved to be photographed. This plate was made in 1899, and its subject was Billy Cramer, 'Riding Champion, Cheyenne Frontier Days'. The city's 'Frontier Days' are still going strong.
COURTESY THE RAINSFORD COLLECTION, WYOMING STATE ARCHIVES AND HISTORICAL DEPARTMENT.

6: Titled 'A Dude has thrown a steer', this photograph was made in Graham County, Arizona, circa 1896-7. Curiously, this 'dude' looks more like the post-Civil War 'Terrible Texan' than did some of the originals!
COURTESY SECRETARY OF THE INTERIOR, NATIONAL ARCHIVES, WASHINGTON, D.C.

1
HOME ON THE RANGE

SIX weeks after the fall of the Alamo in March 1836, Sam Houston's Texans took ferocious revenge on Santa Anna's army in a battle at San Jacinto that lasted scarcely eighteen minutes. Texas was free, but broke. Yet the infant republic was stocked with hard-working, individualistic optimists, and with huge land grants being offered to new settlers, and with vast areas ideally suited for cotton growing, prospects were bright for the new nation that would not be joining the United States until 1845. And then there were the cattle.

7: Cattle king, Charlie Goodnight's ranch.
COURTESY ROBIN MAY COLLECTION.

Almost as soon as news of the bloodbath at San Jacinto spread through Texas, Mexican landowners headed south. At once, there was a straight takeover of their herds by the Anglo-Texans, and the prototype worker of the Western cattle trade, the Texas cowboy, was born. Before tracing his lineage and the origins of the word cowboy, we must examine his debt to the Mexicans he so despised, for it was their Spanish ancestors who had brought cattle – and horses – to the New World in the first place. And the cattle were the ancestors of the lean, mean, moody and magnificent Longhorns that, with the cowboys, were to make history on the Chisholm and other legendary trails.

In 1521, two years after the Conquest of Mexico by Cortez and his conquistadors, a Spanish ship sailed from the island of Hispaniola in the West Indies to Mexico. In it were an unknown number of cattle – one report states that there were six heifers and a young bull – and the shipper was called Gregorio de

Villalobos. They were Andalusian cattle, the breed introduced into the West Indies from Spain in Columbus's day, and from them and later imports stemmed the Longhorns of the American plains.

Horses had crossed to the mainland with Cortez and both were to journey north with Coronado on his great expedition of 1540 in search of the mythical Seven Cities of Gold. Texas saw its first cattle on this expedition, but those that escaped did not populate the area with cows: propagation came a century later. The escaped horses did better, for they and later escapers founded the legion of wild horses which were so to transform the Plains Indians who, until their coming, were footbound.

By the mid-eighteenth century a not insignificant cattle industry was flourishing along the Spanish border from Florida to California. As early as 1715, a French trader named St Denis saw 'thousands of cows, bulls, horses and mares' in Texas, and, later, there were many large ranches, some based on the missions. One mission near Goliad had 40,000 head. And by now animals were being branded, as they were later to

8: An interesting sketch of a bunkhouse. Cowboys had few comforts, but they did like to make their home ranch as 'homelike' as possible.
COURTESY ROBIN MAY COLLECTION.

be, by burning. Even when raiding Apaches, Comanches and other tribes drove off vast numbers of cattle, there were still even wilder ones on the ranges or in the brush. Best organised, perhaps, were the ranches and missions of California, with padres acting as cattlemen, their cowboys being Christian Indians. The mission ranches collapsed when the missions themselves were secularised in 1834. And two years later Texas, though not California, became independent.

The Americans who entered Texas from 1821, led by Stephen Austin, and with Mexican permission, brought cattle of their own so that by 1830 there were around 100,000 cattle in Texas, a fifth of them from the United States, and the two breeds amalgamated to their mutual advantage. And during the Texas Revolution most of them went wild.

9: Stretching out a steer'.
COURTESY THE ERWIN E. SMITH COLLECTION OF RANGE LIFE PHOTOGRAPHS, LIBRARY OF CONGRESS.

The Anglo-Texan takeover that followed the end of the Revolution caused much Mexican bitterness and the bolder Mexicans raided herds in their lost lands for many years. With Indian depradations as well and no market as yet for the Longhorns outside the Republic, the cattle business was not yet a profitable one. But the seeds were being sown, not least in the speed with which the English-speaking Texans mastered the art of tending cows. They might despise the Mexicans, but not their frontier savvy. Before seeing just what that was, however, the word 'cowboy' needs examining.

Enough boys were tending cows on both sides of the Atlantic in the seventeenth century for the word to be in the language as cow-boy, but until recently its origin in a more adult sense was thought to stem from the American Revolution when Tory (Loyalist) guerillas in New York's Westchester County roamed the area stealing Patriot (Rebel) cows and no doubt Loyalist ones as well. They are said to have lured Patriots into traps by tinkling cowbells. Their opposite numbers were called the Skinners, and the picture is confusing enough to make it probable that the word was bandied about to describe thieves, righteous or not, on both sides. However, in his *The First Cowboy*, Charles Zurhurst has traced the word back to the heady days of the Stamp Act and of the Anti-Rent Rebellion in New York colony in 1766. The local landed gentry, known as patroons in that Dutch-colonised area, called their rebellious tenantry 'cow-boys' and meant it very rudely indeed. Space cannot allow us to follow Zurhurst's detailed account of his cowboys and their descendants making their way West to Texas via the Ohio Valley and the Mississippi, but – even allowing for the fact that most Texans originally came from the South – he makes a strong case for his New York, Ohio Valley, Texas chain.

In the early days of the Republic of Texas wild bands of Texans, the most notable of which was led by Ewen Cameron, made life miserable for Indians and, especially, Mexicans, and these reckless riders became known as 'Cowboys' or 'Cameron's Cowboys'. They concerned themselves with Longhorns, too, so it was hardly surprising that the word with the long pedigree settled on the Texas 'cow herder' generally – to use another word that was current in the early days. So were 'stock boy' and 'cow driver', but not yet 'cowpuncher'. Cattleman was always a word for the boss class, along with rancher, stockman and, later, at the top, cattle king and cattle baron.

The Texas cowboys, as noted above, were prepared to use Mexican savvy, if not the name the despised 'greasers' and 'chilli-eaters' went by when they tended cattle – *vaqueros*. The *vaquero*'s clothing, equipment, horse and cattle were either used or adapted by his usurper to a more or lesser degree, as we shall see, though it must be stressed that there were vast herds of wild cattle to which some of those who strayed during the revolution attached themselves. There was nothing wrong with mavericking in these early days, though later the word was to become synonymous with cattle thieving. Samuel Maverick was a lawyer from South Carolina and a signer of the Texas Declaration of Independence. In 1847, he agreed to accept four hundred cattle from a neighbour who owed him $1,200, but seven years later many of them had been stolen or had strayed. So he removed the rest to his ranch on the San Antonio River.

While he was away calves were left unbranded and many cattle strayed, and in 1856, he sold his cattle, land and brand to a rancher named Beauregard, who sent his men out to hunt for strays. They brought in every unbranded cow they could find and burnt them with Maverick's brand. Which is why unbranded and unclaimed cattle became known as mavericks.

When the Civil War broke out, the cattle business was starting to boom, but when the four year struggle ended in 1865 it

10: The Vaquero was a rival but rarely regarded as an equal by the Texans. From a drawing by Frederic Remington.
COURTESY ROBIN MAY COLLECTION.

11: Branding calves – necessary to its owner, but painful for the animal!
COURTESY THE CUNNINGHAM COLLECTION, WESTERN HISTORY COLLECTIONS, UNIVERSITY OF OKLAHOMA LIBRARY.

had virtually collapsed. Even the trail-drive system had developed in the late 1840s and during the 1850s, though only after the war did it achieve spectacular and historic results. The early drives, along with the later, often epic, ones, belong to the next chapter. Here the cowboy's life away from the trail will be described, concentrating on the old days and the open range before barbed wire came and before superior breeds banished the Longhorns into history and legend.

The Texas cowboy therefore deserves, and gets, star billing, along with the reason for his existence: the long-legged and lanky-bodied Longhorn.

The Longhorns that the early cowboys found running wild – and the ones that the next generation found after the chaos of the Civil War – were as tough as they were mean. Blizzards, droughts, Indian arrows and wolves they took in their stride. They were swift wild animals whose horns – up to seven feet tip to tip – were dangerous weapons. Some said they looked sinister and a man who ventured against one on foot was asking for a mauling. Colonel Richard Irving Dodge's testimony is conclusive on the matter: he called the Longhorn 'the domestic animal run wild, changed in some of its habits and characteristics by many generations of freedom and self-care', and noted:

> A footman is never safe when a herd is in his vicinity. Every sportsman who has hunted quail in Texas will have experienced the uneasiness natural to any man around whom a crowd of long-horned beasts are pawing the earth and tossing their heads in anger at his appearance.
>
> I admit some decided frights. On more than one occasion I have felt exceedingly relieved when an aggressive young bull has gone off bellowing and shaking his head, his face full of No. 8 shot, and taking his herd with him. The wild

12: Belligerent, but in his way a beauty. A typical Longhorn steer stares suspiciously at the camera. Note the huge horns – sometimes they grew up to seven feet or more from tip to tip!
COURTESY DENVER PUBLIC LIBRARY WESTERN HISTORY DEPARTMENT.

bull is 'on his muscle' at all times. Though he will generally get out of the way if unmolested, the slightest provocation will convert him into a most aggressive and dangerous enemy.

The wild cattle are not found in herds. A few cows and their calves may associate together for mutual protection, but the bulls are almost always found alone. Should two meet, a most desperate combat determines the mastery then and there, frequently with the life of one of the combatants.

He who would enjoy the favors of a cow must win his way to them by a series of victories. The result of this is that the number of bulls is greatly disproportioned to the number of cows.

And Dodge went on to relate in his *The Hunting Grounds of the Great West* what might be called the ultimate bull Longhorn story. It happened during the American war of 1846-8 against Mexico that was to give California to the United States just as gold was discovered. When General Zachary Taylor's men were on the march from Corpus Christi to Matamoros, one of them fired at a wild bull. The result was staggering:

The bull immediately charged; and the soldier, taking to his heels, ran into the column. The bull, undaunted by the number of his enemies, charged headlong, scattering several regiments like chaff. He finally escaped unhurt, having demoralised and put to flight an army which, a few days later, covered itself with glory by victoriously encountering five times its number of human enemies.

Pitched battles between bulls were desperate affairs:

After much preliminary defiant bellowing, roaring and earth pawing, in the fashion of the buffalo bull, they would pitch into each other with great fury. When one got the advantage of the other, he made the most of it with relentless ferocity, driving his horns deep into the body of his adversary, ripping and tearing, and usually disembowelling him.

To this last account, a later one than Dodge's, should be added the more prosaic but important fact that the Longhorns prospered mightily on their diet of buffalo grass and grama, both of which could survive lengthy droughts and both of which were nourishing in the winter after a summer's broiling. This was to be of decisive importance when the beasts were no longer totally wild. They were that much safer from the hunters in the spring as they hid in dense brush, but mosquitoes drove them from cover in the summer, even their notoriously tough hides being no match for the ferocious insects.

The hunters were taking part in that classic exercise of the range, a roundup, though in the early days it was usually called

13: Before any drive could take place there were many chores to be done. Here we see an initial roundup and sorting of cattle ready for branding.
COURTESY NEBRASKA STATE HISTORICAL SOCIETY.

a cow drive or a cow hunt. But before sending our Texas cowboy out on one, he deserves a full description, some of which, but not all, fits his more northerly fellow hired hands.

The Texas cowboy was usually a first or second generation Texan of Southern stock. He wanted adventure and excitement rather than money, which was just as well as his pay was normally around thirty dollars a month. That much of his work was dirty and monotonous was something he accepted unless he had visions of life as an outlaw. The chances were that he was of Scotch-Irish stock, ie. Protestant, though Teddy Blue assures us that most cowboys, the vast majority, were 'infidels'. He was a proud man and after the war a bitter one. The natural tension between cowtown lawmen and the cowboys was the result of defeated men clashing with Northern peace officers. For a Southerner – who would allow himself to be 'tamed' by a Texas Ranger – it was a disgrace to be locked up by a damned Yankee, a bluebelly bastard.

The cowboy, northern or southern, worked hard and uncomplainingly. His loyalty to his boss and his friends is heavily

documented, as is his generosity to his friends. Decent women filled him with awe and total respect, and he was courageous and self-reliant: he had to be. He treated his horses better than Mexicans or Indians treated theirs.

He was not very talkative, indeed, anyone in the cattle country on the gabby side was liable to be advised: 'Save part of your breath for breathing.' He rarely used his fists for fighting and tended to despise those that did: soldiers, freighters etc. His marksmanship, however, with his chosen weapon, the six-shooter, was rarely good enough to take on a genuine gunfighter on either side of the law. His sense of humour was strong, though sometimes extreme. When Baylis John Fletcher was going *Up the Trail in '79*, the name of his excellent book, he and the other cowboys halted for the night beside the Guadalupe River, in which they saw a big alligator. The beast vanished into the muddy depths when the men started shouting at it; then it was time for dinner:

> After dinner Joe Felder took off his boots and washed his feet in the river. There he sat on the root of a big tree facing the stream and fell asleep. Manuel Garcia, our Cook, with that levity characteristic of the Mexican, conceived a practical joke. Throwing a log so that it fell into the river just in front of the sleeping Joe, he shouted, 'Alligator!' In a quick effort to rise, Joe slipped into the river, going entirely under and rising by the side of the floating log, which he mistook for the alligator. He screamed for help, and stake ropes were thrown to him, which he seized frantically to be drawn out, as he thought from the jaws of death. His disgust was profound when he discovered that he was escaping only from a rotten log.

A greenhorn and a tenderfoot were always fair game and it was a good laugh if one fell off a horse and dislocated a shoulder, while a whole trainload of greenhorns once watched in horror as some cowboys staged a cruel piece of theatre. They had made a

14: Remington's drawings graphically portray the daily life and style of dress of the cowboy.
COURTESY ROBIN MAY COLLECTION.

dummy man, filled 'him' with grass and, as the train drew up, strung him up on the crossbar of a telegraph pole. At once the boys commenced shooting at the swinging figure, then they shot the rope in half and down came the dummy. Away rode one of the boys, pulling the apparent victim, while the rest filled the bounding body with lead. The appalled onlookers urged the conductor to pull out before the train itself was held up, and pull out it did, with children screaming and women fainting and the boys laughing fit to bust.

The cowboy's prejudices were legion. As noted, he cordially disliked Mexicans, though there were plenty on the range in the Southwest. There were a number of black cowboys, but though they were accepted by the Anglo-Americans as working partners, they did not share a bunkhouse or social life in town. Not all cowboys hated Indians, or considered them 'gut eaters' (ie eaters of beef entrails) or just plain varmints (vermin). Indeed Teddy Blue admired the Cheyennes and married one of cattle-baron Granville Stuart's pretty half-Shoshone daughters, agreeing with his friend, the artist Charlie Russell, who was also a cowboy as well as an 'Injun-lover'. 'God, I wish I'd been a Sioux Indian a hundred years ago,' Teddy said to Russell, who replied that the Sioux had been living in heaven for a thousand years 'and we took it away from 'em for forty dollars a month.' Cowboys were never as much 'white Indians' as the Mountain Men who trapped beaver a generation or more before them, but they shared a love of freedom, and some cowboys at least sympathised with the 'varmints'.

15: Cowboys were noted for comradeship, and an injured companion could rely on their help.
COURTESY KANSAS STATE HISTORICAL SOCIETY.

They rarely sympathised with townspeople, at least the Kansas variety they met in the cowtowns, and could not even feel much affection for cotton-picking Texans. As for settlers, 'sodbusters' was too polite a word for mere squatters, clodbusters, wool-hat people, nesters . . .

Texan cowboys tended to criticise those unfortunate enough to work elsewhere, especially in the matter of clothing and equipment, and the feelings were mutual. California's cowboys looked too Mexican for a Texan's taste, while the woolly chaps and the overalls of northern cowboys excited his scorn. The Northerners had plenty of jokes to tell about primitive Texans, including the one about the Texas cowboy who came to dinner at a northern roundup camp and was passed the sugar. 'No thanks. I don't take salt in my coffee,' said the Texan who had never been introduced to sugar before.

But at least all cowboys were united in their detestation of sheepmen and their stinking, bleating woollies who ruined the grass of the range, and fouled waterholes. No decent cowboy would soil his lips with mutton and many a sheepherder and his charges were to be killed before cattle and sheep managed to share the West together. There was a vicious attack on sheepmen in Wyoming as late as 1909, three being killed.

The first thing a cowboy sleeping on the prairie tended to do when he woke was put on his hat. The most popular type was the wide-brimmed stetson (named after J. B. Stetson, the hat-

16: A Kansas bunkhouse in the 1880s or 1890s on a ranch in Clark County.
COURTESY KANSAS STATE HISTORICAL SOCIETY.

maker), which had a relatively high crown, and which protected him against wind, rain, hail, snow and the sun. Its nickname, the ten gallon hat, was not just due to its size but because a man or a horse could use it for drinking. It was creased or not according to taste.

The bandanna round his neck prevented sunburn and mopped up sweat when required, while it could be used to protect the nose and mouth from trail dust. It could also help ward off frostbite in the fierce blizzards of the northern ranges.

Shirts were of flannel or cotton and collarless and, unless the weather was very hot, the hand wore long johns. His woollen pants fitted tight to his waist because braces (suspenders) were uncomfortable when working, as was a belt. He carried his tobacco for his cigarettes in his deep vest (waistcoat) pockets,

17: A posed but necessary scene at any ranch. Here a cowboy demonstrates the importance of his lariat. With it he can skilfully 'cut out' a particular cow or steer or calf from the herd, frequently from the back of a galloping horse. COURTESY NEBRASKA STATE HISTORICAL SOCIETY.

which, unlike pants pockets, could be used when a man was riding. Some cowboys wore gloves, others scorned them.

The boots a cowboy wore were of Spanish origin and their sloping, underslung heels kept his feet firmly against the stirrups. And his spurs, too, whose jinglebobs made him jingle as he walked along (when he had to dismount) were very like a *vaquero*'s. However, they were less cruel. The points on the stars of his rowels were not sharp, being merely for show. Similarly, the Anglo-American cowboy did not use the painful spade bit to be found in the mouths of Mexican horses. Wooden block stirrups used by *vaqueros* gave way to bent-wood gear which were lighter.

The cowboys were quite prepared to use the *chaparejos* or

chaparreras of their southern counterparts. Written as chaps but pronounced shaps, these were leather leg protectors, some being the shotgun style, which were close-fitting, the others being wide 'batwing' chaps. There were also the woolly chaps used on the northern ranges. Chaps were only really needed in brush country, but they were as much a part of a cowboy's outfit as his hat. In thick brush country protection was vital. Teddy Blue had a terrifying experience when a thunderclap set off a stampede one night. He leapt up from sleep and jumped on his horse without putting on his chaps – and spent much of the night chasing the herd through thorny brush. The result was a face covered in blood, hands cut to pieces – he had left his gloves in his chaps pocket – and a great hole in his forehead. He was picking the thorns out all the way to Kansas and, not

18: An outlaw steer (or bull) could be a real problem. Here four cowboys have successfully got one under control – and one has a tail hold on him!
COURTESY KANSAS STATE HISTORICAL SOCIETY.

having the inborn love of the brush country of many of the Texans, he swore an oath directed at the boss: 'If God Almighty ever lets me out of this brush, I'm never going back into it.' He never did, Montana becoming his final home.

The Texan cowboy preferred a shorter *reata* or rope than that used by Mexicans or Californians. Theirs were sixty feet long, but his lariat was twenty-five to thirty-five feet and made of fibre, not braided rawhide. But he adapted the Mexican saddle to his use, a saddle that itself descended directly from the Spanish war saddle of the sixteenth century, which in turn had been adapted from even earlier Moorish saddles. The big horn was used to secure a lariat; Texans tied the rope to the horn, unlike the Mexicans who simply secured it by a couple of twists. Adaptations included the tilting back of the cantle for comfort on long rides – the old Spanish ones had been tilted sharply forward to secure armoured troops in position, though later Spaniards and Mexicans had begun to tilt them back. Also the Texans chose open reins, not the closed reins of the Mexicans. This was because a cowboy often had to ground-tie his horse, which meant simply to drop his reins on the ground of

19.

the treeless plains or prairies. His horse was trained to stand anchored on the spot.

If a cowboy's saddle, hat and boots were the most important and cherished items of his equipment, his six-gun was just as essential even if it spent much of its time in working periods in his bedroll. That did not mean it was not well looked after, though a legend has grown up that many pistols were rusty from lack of use. It was not often worn at work for the obvious reason that it was in the way, though on the trail north it was in place on the hip. The chances were that it was a .44 or .45 calibre single-action Colt Peacemaker from the 1870s, though during the late 1890s fewer and fewer men automatically packed a gun, though most cowboys owned one. There were exceptions to the housing of firearms in bedrolls on the range, of course, notably when the Comanches were still raiding in Texas. The last of them were put on reservations outside Texas in the '70s.

As for rifles, which the hand was likely to shoot much more accurately than a Colt – only experts could use pistols accurately beyond close range – it was likely from the mid-'70s to be a Winchester '73 model, until the '94 carbine proved even better. But it must be stressed that – except in wild and woolly cowtowns, especially in their early days – there was not much gunfire on

19: The interior of Sawtell's Ranch in 1872. The assorted weapons may look decorative, but they are all strategically placed!
COURTESY WYOMING STATE ARCHIVES AND HISTORICAL DEPARTMENT.

20: Cowboys around the campfire relaxing and fooling around with their pistols for the benefit of the camera man.
COURTESY WYOMING STATE ARCHIVES AND HISTORY DEPARTMENT.

the range. As one old-timer remarked: 'There was a hell of a lot more post holes dug . . . than guns shot off.'

'Unlike the lot of Gilbert and Sullivan's policeman, the cowboy's life was a happy one,' Richard Dillon has written, and there is plenty of evidence that most cowboys liked the job. Before he died, Earle R. Forrest, the Pennsylvanian historian and journalist, and expert on the Southwest, recalled for Joseph Rosa some memories of his days as a cowboy at the turn of the century:

> The old open range days was a great life. It was hard, that is the work was hard and dangerous and you had to stand all kinds of weather, but in the winter we were generally at the

home ranch or in a snug line cabin somewhere on the range. . . . It was a great life, and we all loved it. I disliked the rainy season more than snow and the cold weather when we were out with the wagon. Of course we slept on the ground. Each had his own bed made of a heavy canvas wagon sheet about 14 feet long and seven feet wide. We would make up a bed of blankets and soughans (comforts) on one half and then pull the rest of the canvas sheet up over that. Of course . . . if it rained that night, well, you just got good and wet. The canvas tarp kept you pretty dry on top, but the water had a habit of running along the ground and under you and soaking up through everything. Like everything else you got used to that in time. When it snowed it was much more comfortable because the snow formed a protective covering over you, and it was kind of warm. . . . It sure was a great life and I never knew a cowboy of the old open range that didn't love it.

Love it despite that rain! Love it despite the fact that one was looking after dumb critters, often on an empty sea of grass. It was a hard life of routine work, but though few enjoyed regular doses of adventure or excitement, the work was not monotonous. If trail herding was the high spot of the early cowboy's existence, the chief events of the year on the ranch were the spring and fall roundups. After the trail-driving days the spring roundup was for branding calves, the fall for gathering beeves for shipment to market and branding any new arrivals or any calves missed earlier. But in the early days in the Southwest the spring roundup, apart from branding new calves, was for

21: 'A hot iron and a sharp knife'. COURTESY THE ERWIN E. SMITH COLLECTION OF RANGE LIFE PHOTOGRAPHS, LIBRARY OF CONGRESS.

22: On home ranges as well as on the trail, it was necessary to hobble the cow ponies each night. But once saddled and bridled, most of them would stand for hours if their owner 'ground hitched' the reins.
COURTESY KANSAS STATE HISTORICAL SOCIETY.

gathering mature beef – four years old or more – for the drive north.

Between roundups, the twice-yearly cattle harvests, when a cowboy wasn't driving wild cattle from their hiding places, he could hope to go mustanging. This was lively work for it meant hunting down wild horses – bands of mares ruled by a stallion. A cowhand went after the mustangs not at the gallop, as in films and foolish fiction, but steadily until he tired the animals out. After luring them into a pen or a blind trap – fortunately mustangs tended to like to return to a favourite range – he hobbled them with forked sticks tied just below the ankles, the hobbles being called clogs. Any cowboy foolish enough to opt for speed rather than steadiness was likely to ruin his saddle horse and his quarry as well.

There was little or nothing to do in the winter and most cowhands were paid off. Some were kept on, good hands being valuable, but for several months they got no pay, there being no work for them to do. However, they got free board, while others wandered round the ranches on the range at each of which they would be given a meal. The law of hospitality was sacred in the West. A hand might get himself a job for the next season in this way, but if he carried on claiming hospitality into the working season, though he would still be given it, he would become known as a saddle tramp.

Those with money to spare and the inclination would whoop it up in town until their money ran out. If few towns equalled the Kansas cowtowns in their gaudy prime, which will be described in Chapter Three, there were plenty of other spots where a man could go wild in winter or summer alike. And if he had spent the time on a ranch he would be feeling dry, for no cattleman allowed drinking and precious few gambling. The bosses wanted peace.

Wildness included frolics with firearms. It was considered good fun to shoot the end off someone's pipe or his cigar at close range in the bar. Parking your shooting irons tended to be the rule only where tough lawmen were faced with potentially explosive situations day after day, not when the main problem was high spirits.

The local sporting girls ('soiled doves') had more independence than they would have had in brothels back East. The hard cases in Kansas cowtowns will be described more fully in Chapter Three, but it is worth remarking here that whores and cowboys usually got along fine. There were women the boys

23: 'Hey, keep your mind on the job – that's my neck you're a choppin' at!' Cowboys rarely found time to visit barbers, and despite the distraction of the camera, this one at least can be sure of a trim.
COURTESY THE PHILLIPS COLLECTION, WESTERN HISTORY COLLECTIONS, UNIVERSITY OF OKLAHOMA LIBRARY.

would never touch, but they could console the louse-ridden buffalo-hunters – while they were still around – who never changed their heavy clothes. A cowboy might attract lice, but he didn't want it that way and enjoyed a good clean-up and a new outfit at the end of a trail, but the buffalo hunter gloried in his filth – or so the cowboys said. They also claimed on the northern range that soldiers got a woman when she'd left the dogs.

One of the most constructive winter jobs was becoming a wolfer. As wolves could each kill around seventy-five cattle a year, ranchers were prepared to hire cowboys to shoot or poison them, paying up to ten dollars for each victim and sometimes a bounty as well. The trick was not to try and run the big beast down but hang around his lair and get him when he was slowed down by food. Then it was a case of crawling into the lair with a six-gun and a candle and strong nerves, for the explosion blew the candle out.

The cowboy's day started around 4am in summer. The chances were that he would be sleeping in the open in his bedroll if he was hot, bunkhouses being a compound of lice, bedbugs, clothes scattered everywhere and a general vista of untidiness, plus a smell that was a mixture of sweat, cow dung, boots and the liquorice in chewing tobacco. In his evocatively named autobiography, *A Texas Cow Boy or, Fifteen Years on the Hurricane Deck of a Spanish Pony*, published in 1885, and the first of many cowboy memoirs, Charlie Siringo recalled how the boys in his bunkhouse had a rule that 'whoever was caught picking grey backs [lice] off and throwing them on the floor without first killing them, should pay a fine of ten cents for each and every offense'. The fines went to pay for 'choice literature',

24: The day's chores started with the selection of a horse from the remuda. Here is yet another use for the cowboy's all-purpose lariat.
COURTESY ROBIN MAY COLLECTION.

which meant picture magazines and mail-order catalogues as a rule.

The bedroll was a Victorian version of a sleeping bag and was a tarpaulin – a 'tarp' – with flaps, and in it a cowboy felt warm and cozy. He could put blankets or a buffalo robe in it and into it also went his 'war bag', which contained his few belongings: his six-gun and ammunition, a razor, perhaps a picture of his family.

If he was on the prairie – a word he liked though he was usually on the Plains – he would get his hat on first, as already noted, dress, if he wasn't already dressed, then head for the chuck wagon. The cook or Cookie – often known as the Coosie (from the Spanish *cocinero*) – would already have yelled an exhortation like 'Come and git it or I'll throw it out', and it behoved the cowboy to obey, Coosie being an important personage on the range or up the trail. Before breakfast a man might dash a little water across his face and would probably scratch himself, as he walked bandily along, to try and evict his travelling companions, lice and fleas. Not that he accepted them, like Indians or, as noted, buffalo hunters, but the chances of a bath were not frequent. No wonder he got a new outfit in town at the end of a trail drive and had a hot tub. And, ordinarily, he would try and bathe when possible, boil his clothes occasionally, or dry-clean them over an ant-hill.

He was only happy doing mounted work, but sometimes water had to be carried and – from the 1880s – fence posts had to be set up and barbed wire attached to them.

The chances were that the day would start with a call at the *remuda*. This was the horse herd awaiting saddling and work,

25: 'A real cutting horse turning on a dime.' These animals were able to out-think and outrun even the most 'ornery' of 'critters'. COURTESY THE ERWIN E. SMITH COLLECTION OF RANGE LIFE PHOTOGRAPHS, LIBRARY OF CONGRESS.

26: This photograph of Ned Coy, a Dakota cowboy, was made in 1888, and was described as 'limbering up on Boy Dick.' COURTESY NEBRASKA STATE HISTORICAL SOCIETY.

and looked after by the wrangler, the most menial hand, but a good way for a likely lad to get started. Each cowboy was allocated eight to a dozen horses for his own personal use, and no one, not even a boss, could use one of them without permission. These small saddle horses were all geldings and they got plenty of personal attention, as befitted friends who were partners in the task of looking after the cattle. The best of them developed a rare instinct for rounding up beef and cutting out steers. Breaking horses was usually left to bronc busters, for it was a highly skilled job. The breaking usually occurred at four years old, sometimes at five.

There was plenty to do on the range minding the cattle and keeping them fit. One of the worst jobs was riding bog – rescuing cows from the mire or quicksands. A two-man team went to work and were often rewarded for their efforts by an infuriated Longhorn coming at them with his vicious horns.

Everything stopped for a prairie fire, which could ruin the grass for months or even years. To help prevent fires spreading

27: Remington's descriptive drawing of a bucking bronco was published in the 1890s and many an old (and young) cowboy who saw it must have mentally relived the jolts and jars experienced when trying to tame a wild horse.
COURTESY ROBIN MAY COLLECTION.

28: Line riders encamped outside their dugout, from a drawing by Frederic Remington.
COURTESY ROBIN MAY COLLECTION.

firebreaks were ploughed at intervals, with the grass burnt off between them. Fire-fighting was made worse by the fact that a sandstorm might be pushing the fire and adding searing pain to the smoke. Sometimes a drag made of a wet tarp or wagon sheet, weighed down by fence posts, was pulled along just ahead of the line of fire to wet the area and the first advancing flames, and if such a drag could not be constructed, a heifer was killed, then slit open from throat to tail below. Its ribs would be broken and two riders would drag it flat along the ground, trying to make the bloody mass quench the flames. The horses had to change sides continually to prevent their hooves getting burnt.

A more mundane task was anointing the wounds on cattle made by blowflies laying eggs that turned into screw-worms. Bottles of carbolic acid mixed with axle grease and other 'potions' were carried round the range in the summer to combat the menace.

In the early days, overgrazing, overstocking and, of course, drought could kill a range, and cowboys had to drive their charges to new ranges. Later, windmills and barbed wire – which themselves needed looking after – made moves less vital, the windmills providing enough water in tanks.

Riding line in summer or, especially, winter was the worst chore that a cowboy had to endure. When barbed wire came it became 'riding fence'. Big ranches had to have line camps, outposts on the extremities of the range where a man, or, possibly, two men, patrolled a beat of perhaps fifteen or more miles. He or the pair lived in a shack or a dugout but it was most likely to be a solo assignment. It was a hermit-like existence, the hand ensuring that cattle did not stray and that other brands stayed out, and keeping a wary eye out for rustlers, outlaws or wild animals. He also had to see that cows avoided alkaline water. Ramon Adams has described the life as that of a 'buck nun', though some lucky lineman might strike up an acquaintance with a (normally to be despised) sodbuster, who might even have a daughter. At least riding line was better than riding fence as one's route on patrol could be varied more.

29: Counting cattle before a drive; Texas cowboys at the turn of the century.
COURTESY THE ERWIN E. SMITH COLLECTION OF RANGE LIFE PHOTOGRAPHS, LIBRARY OF CONGRESS.

Worst of all, the line man might miss one of the rare parties back at the ranch, and if the ranch was a big one such parties might have real live decent women. Cowboys dancing with cowboys, 'heifer-branded' by an apron or other mark of femininity, was not the same thing at all. Meanwhile, back at the line camp . . . one unfortunate cowboy incarcerated all winter at a Texas horse camp, was found by his friends the following spring shooting at a stump on which were draped his hat and coat. Said the lonesome cowhand: 'I'm going to get the son of a bitch before he gets me!'

And then there were the round-ups . . .

Just as he popularised the word 'cowboy' and made it an admirable one, so Buffalo Bill Cody made a household word out of 'round-up'. He gave a straightforward account of one in his (genuine) autobiography of 1879, written before his great days as a showman had got past the one-night stand stage:

> The word round-up is derived from the fact that during the winter months the cattle become scattered over a vast track of land, and the ranchmen assemble together in the spring to sort out and each secure his own stock. They form a large circle, often of a circumference of two hundred miles, and drive the cattle towards a common centre, where, all the stock being branded, each owner can readily separate his own from the general herd, and then he drives them to his

30: Cowboys constructing a 'rope corral' for their horses.
COURTESY ROBIN MAY COLLECTION.

own ranch. In this cattle driving business is exhibited some most magnificent horsemanship, for the 'cow-boys', as they are called, are invariably skillful and fearless horsemen – in fact only a most expert rider could be a cow-boy, as it requires the greatest dexterity and daring in the saddle to cut a wild steer out of the herd . . . there is nothing but hard work on these round-ups, having to be in the saddle all day, and standing guard over the cattle at night, rain or shine. [But] it was an exciting life, and the days sped rapidly by; in six weeks we found ourselves at our own ranch on Dismal river, the round-up having proved a great success, as we had found all our cattle and driven them home.

Naturally, with the coming of barbed wire, roundups were comparatively simple affairs compared with the old days when a single one could spread over thousands of miles. The stockmen cooperated because it was common sense to do so, besides

31: A sketch depicting cowboys cutting out calves and keeping an eye on the irate cows.
COURTESY ROBIN MAY COLLECTION.

which it was a marvellous bi-annual get together. In overall charge was an elected roundup captain, a Napoleonic figure to whom all deferred, cattle owners included. Assuming the operation was a big one, he appointed a number of lieutenants. The local cattlemen shared the expense of the operation depending on how many head they owned as to how much they paid, and each of them provided a roundup crew, the bigger ones having up to fifty hands and their own chuck wagon. Each area was worked in turn until every owner had harvested his stock.

Each 'wagon' taking part in the roundup – wagon being the roundup crew from an individual ranch – was led by a wagon boss. The cook had a helper called a swamper and there was also a wrangler and a night wrangler, who was known as the nighthawk. The riders who set out with the boss formed a big circle at the centre of which was the next campsite where the cook sited the chuck wagon. The riders' job was to flush out cattle from clumps of trees, the brush, draws and timber, then head them towards the centre of the circle. With them rode one or two 'reps' or representatives of nearby ranches whose job it was to cut out stock belonging to their own ranches. Reps enjoyed independence though they needed good memories, for they were expected to know every brand, earmark and

32: Branding activity on the JA Ranch: here the cowboys have sorted the cattle into pens.
COURTESY PANHANDLE-PLAINS HISTORICAL MUSEUM.

wattle mark (on the neck or the jaw) over a wide area.

When the cattle reached the centre of the circle, they would be cut (segregated). Then those which had to be branded or castrated would take their painful turn at the branding fire.

'Cutting out' was a skilled art. Everett Dick described it succinctly in the Collections of the Kansas State Historical Society Vol. XVII (1926-28) in his *The Long Drive:*

> It required skilled cowboys and skilled cow ponies. Two cowboys worked together in order to accomplish the most with the minimum effort. When a beef was selected he was manoeuvred adroitly to the edge of the herd. At the opportune time a dash was made at him and before he knew it he was on the outside. When he discovered this, he made a desperate attempt to regain the herd, and all of the cowboy's skill was then required to keep him from doing so. One man rode behind the steer and another beside him. As long as there was any chance of outrunning his pursuers, the steer persisted, but seeing no chance for a further attempt, he turned and joined a group of his comrades that had been cut out before and were being held a few rods distant. In the beginning of the 'cut out' a few gentle cows or work oxen were driven a short distance from the 'round up' herd. These served as a nucleus, and the 'cut out' steers joined them. 'Cutting out' was done in the open on a level prairie and never in a corral as was done on the northern farm, or is usually done at the present time. A Texas drover, even in the North, always preferred the open to a corral of any kind. He did not, however, want to do anything with cattle while on foot. He was justified in his inclinations in this matter, for a Texas steer, when coralled, usually became belligerent and would

33: A drawing made in the early 1870s of a typical cutting and branding scene on a Texas ranch.
COURTESY ROBIN MAY COLLECTION.

34: **Branding on a Nebraska ranch.**
COURTESY NEBRASKA STATE HISTORICAL SOCIETY.

> make a dash for anyone on foot. Often in loading cattle on a car, an animal would be separated from the herd and he would fight every time. Many times a northern man, who was accustomed to handling cattle on foot, walked into a stockyard and was suddenly faced by a steer with an arched back, downset head, distended nostrils, and glaring eyes, charging at him. The result was that he had to run for the nearest fence as fast as he could go.

The good cutting horse was the most admired horse in cattle country. After the cutting out, the cows that needed branding were brought down by the skilled combination of cowboy, lariat and cow pony, or a pair of each, then it was time for some wrestling with the frightened calves, two of the boys holding a victim down, another wielding the hot iron and, perhaps, a fourth nicking its ear for extra identification.

The male calf had to endure castration, a tricky job as the new steer was liable to be infected by screw-worms.

Barring accidents, most of the roundup techniques presented no problems to skilled men, but the exception was roping which was always potentially dangerous. Apart from the chance of heavy falls, there was always the possibility of losing a thumb or a finger, sliced off because a rider had carelessly hitched his rope round the saddle horn, then a maddened steer had pulled it taut. Teddy Blue quoted a Mexican who criticised the way Montana cowboys dallied (half hitched their loops), badly, unlike Texans, and a footnote reveals that Montana and Wyoming were both full in the 1930s of cowboys with thumbs and fingers missing.

At the end of the roundup the reps, walking encyclopedias of the range's brands even though some of them could not read, would take their own cattle back to their ranches. Though pictures show the early Longhorns going up the trail with their horns in all their glory, it soon became the practice to dehorn outsize ones which could inflict grievous injuries on other cows. Clippers and saws did the job and, meanwhile, tallymen chosen by the roundup captain were responsible for noting all the calves branded. There were often mavericks and dogies (calves separated from their mothers), also branded strays from so far away that there were no reps to claim them. It was hardly worth a special drive home for the strays, so they were driven off with the main herd and their owners were credited on a 'strays account'.

35: Dehorning cattle on a ranch in Clark County Kansas. Early drives up from Texas were composed of Longhorn cattle – with spreads of up to seven feet – but later, for safety and to save space in cattle cars, some owners dehorned the beasts first.
COURTESY KANSAS STATE HISTORICAL SOCIETY.

Night after night during roundup the boys settled down at Cookie's new camp and, hopefully, their cook was one of the good ones. At least there was always beef on the hoof to hand, but no one, not even the boss, could take the cook for granted. We will meet him again and more fully in the next chapter and leave the cowboys to settle down for the night, though, as on the trail, they had to take their turn at night guard. The wranglers put their charges behind a rope corral, the night wrangler getting in a little sleep before he went on guard. The perils were minimal compared to those of the trail, though stampedes inevitably occurred on the range. But the full dramatic and sometimes tragic impact of them is best told as part of the story of the trail drives out of Texas, and to set the scene for the drives, let us end with a quote from the *Galveston News* on 16 August, 1866, a year after the Civil War had ended. The roundup, or the cow hunt as it was still called, had become an obsession with the youth of Texas:

> There is not a boy of American parentage learning a trade or reading for a profession west of the Colorado. Our youths have souls above the mechanical arts. The little children, as early as they can walk, pilfer their mother's tape and make lassos to rope the kittens and the ducks. The boys, as soon as they can climb on a pony, are off to the prairie to drive stock. As they advance toward manhood, their highest ambition is to conquer a pitching mustang or throw a wild beef by the tail.

So the defeated Southern state of Texas prepared for the new challenge in the North.

36: Remington's drawing of a branded steer suggests that the actual brand or letter was bigger than it really was.
COURTESY ROBIN MAY COLLECTION.

Charlie Siringo's autobiography, mentioned in the chapter above, has many useful facts about life on the range. Here are some of them:

A cowboy's outfit is something like a Boston dude's rig, it can be bought for a small sum or large amount according to the purchasers' means and inclinations.

If you wish to put on style and at the same time have a serviceable outfit, you can invest $50 very handy; this is by going or sending to Texas or old Mexico, the only place where such costly outfits are kept.

Your saddle would cost $100 although the Mexicans have them as high as $300. Another $50 for a gold mounted Mexican sombrero (hat). And $100 for a silver mounted bridle and spurs to match. Now a $50 saddle-blanket to match your saddle and another $25 for a squirt (quirt) and 'Re-etta' (raw-hide rope). Your Colts '45' pearl-handled gold-mounted pistol would cost $50, a Winchester to match, $75 and $25 for a pair of Angora goat leggings, making a total of $475 leaving $25 out of the $500 to buy a Spanish buggy with.

Years ago costly outfits were worn by nearly all Cow-men but this day and age are seldom indulged . . . now-days it requires more rough and tumble hard work than skill to command good wages on a cattle ranch. Cattle are becoming so tame from being bred with short horns that it requires but very little skill and knowledge to be a Cow-boy . . .

Well now for the cost of a common outfit, with a few words of advice to the young tender-foot who wishes to become a Cow-boy.

Mount a Railroad and go to any of the large 'shipping' or 'cattle-towns', – then purchase a cheap pony, for about $25; saddle for $25; leather leggings for $50; broad-brim White-hat for $10; saddle-bags which would do to sleep on also $50. Another $5 for spurs, bridle, stake-rope etc.

And now for the most important ornament the old reliable '45' Pistol Colts, $12. If you are foolish enough to go without the latter, the cooks at the different ranches where you happen to stop will not respect you. . . .

2

UP THE TRAIL

THE Longhorns got bad press notices when they hit New York. New York? Not only did the great beasts get driven there, but they reached the city in the 1850s, a decade before the spectacular trail drives began. Beady-eyed Manhattan buyers were not impressed. Said the *New York Times*: 'According to the opinions of the sellers, they would not weigh anything were it not for their horns, which were useful in preventing them from crawling through fences.' That was in 1858, and whether the beeves had been walked all the way or transported by rail from Illinois, they were not much admired. No doubt some would have agreed with the observer in a St Louis stockyard who in 1857 told the *Missouri Republican* that Longhorns were not fit for people to eat but 'will do to bait traps to catch wolves in.' Times were to change. . . .

In the early years of the Texas Republic there was not much demand for beef at home or abroad, though prices were to rise from some five dollars per head for stock cattle and twice as much for fat beeves around 1850 to twenty a head for five beeves a decade later. Yet even as early as 1836, while the Battle of San Jacinto was being fought, a herd was being driven eastwards to New Orleans. The 1840s saw cattle being trailed

37: A Texas herd of Longhorns on the trail, from a painting by Frederic Remington.
COURTESY KANSAS STATE HISTORICAL SOCIETY.

northwards to Missouri, to Ohio, and in growing numbers to Louisiana and New Orleans, but it was the cattle drives to California, after gold had been discovered by James Marshall at Sutter's Mill in 1848, that saw the true start of cattle drives on a large scale.

It is a mainly forgotten start, for all too often the story of the drives out of Texas is made to begin after the Civil War. The demand in California was a very real one, which came at a time when supply was exceeding demand in Louisiana. And it took a particularly rugged breed of men to get the cattle through to the miners, for the early part of the route lay across scorching deserts and through Apache country. After the Apaches came the threat of warring Yumas and Mohaves, but once beyond the

38: Riders moving among a milling herd and hastening them on by the use of a quirt. From a drawing by Remington.
COURTESY ROBIN MAY COLLECTION.

Colorado and into California the journey north became a comparative pleasure.

Trailing to California – the peak came in 1854 – was always a major gamble. The human enemies, the scalding winds and lack of grass and water in the deserts, the poisonous weeds and alkaline lakes, and the appalling trails, killed off many animals, while prices in California could vary wildly. One year a drover might buy cattle from a rancher at $15 a head in Texas and get $150 a head at journey's end, the next he might be lucky to get $25 a head and lose a small fortune at the hands of the Apaches. Yet the cattle – an economic number of them – survived the extreme perils of the California route and it became clear to cattlemen that a direct route northwards through northern Texas and the Indian Territory to Missouri and points beyond would be much less of a risk because of the better grass. So the first great trail out of Texas was born: the Shawnee Trail to Kansas City, which had replaced New Orleans as the chief market for Texas beef by the start of the Civil War in 1861. Missourians, New Yorkers and others might sneer at the Longhorns, but the thousands of emigrants heading across the plains for California were glad of their meat, and so were the masses that followed them after the war, not least the flood of emigrants from Europe for whom tough Longhorn meat was an undoubted improvement on what most of them were used to back home.

Before the war began a most unwelcome plague had made its appearance in the cattle country, a disease that was to have a considerable effect on the history of the trade. So before setting the Longhorns in motion up the most famous trail of all, the Chisholm, after the Civil War, it is time to introduce the tick that carried the fever known as Texas, Mexican or Spanish fever.

As it happened, no one knew that the tick was the carrier in the early years of the trail-driving age, though the Longhorns, which were indeed housing the fat, blood-bloated insects, got the blame for infecting northern cattle with a disease to which they themselves were immune. The Longhorns carried countless ticks up the trails and the parasites would fall off and later prey on northern herds that could not resist their virus. The wretched beasts rapidly sickened with the fever, many of them dying. Others were hopelessly weakened and so ill and lethargic that it took months to get them into marketable shape again. Various theories were advanced by scientists about the disease, a few guessing correctly that the ticks were the carriers, but there could be no denying that the Longhorns were responsible in some way for an annual disaster that only ended with the coming of cold weather. (In 1868 an English scientist, John Gamgee, was to diagnose the plague for the U.S. Commissioners of Agriculture. Later, dealers were to pay compensation for dead cattle, which was to help reduce tensions.)

In June, 1859, almost a year before the Civil War, the *Missouri Weekly Sentinel* reported an incident which anticipated later events:

Texas Fever. – Three droves of Texas cattle, numbering in all some two thousand, attempted to pass through our county on Saturday last, but were stopped . . . by committee appointed by the recent Bellmont convention. This course of proceeding may be considered illegal, but our farmers have their rights as well as the Texas drovers, and no intelligent person who is at all conversant with the past history of stockraising in this county can for a moment blame the citizens of Missouri for adopting summary measures to protect their stock from the fearful ravages of Spanish fever.

39: Oliver Loving, whose partnership with Goodnight proved so short yet memorable.
COURTESY THE DENVER PUBLIC LIBRARY, WESTERN HISTORY DEPARTMENT.

The 1850s saw the first quarantine regulations against the fever but, as the Longhorns were unaffected themselves, they were ineffective. So farmers took direct action, turning back the cattle and demanding tougher legislation. The upshot was a measure barring Southern cattle from four Kansas counties in 1859 and the first trail to Colorado by Oliver Loving in 1860. We shall be meeting him again.

In 1861 Missouri brought in a quarantine law, but now the inevitable war broke out and, on 19 April, Lincoln banned trade with the South. There was a small amount of unofficial trading between Texans and Kansans and some forays by Kansas to steal Southern cows, but the main occupation of those cattlemen and cowboys not in uniform was feeding the Southern armies – with routes shrinking after the Union gained control of the Mississippi in 1863. True, some daring drovers swam their herds across the river below Vicksburg, risking discovery by Union gunboats, but the money they made – Confederate money – was valueless when the war ended in 1865. Others actually sold beeves to the victorious occupiers of New Orleans despite strong protests from Confederate leaders.

The end of the war found Texas cattlemen in dire straits. Drought had killed thousands of cattle and few wanted to buy the survivors. Meanwhile, thousands more were grazing unbranded and virtually wild on the open range. Ranches were run down; the defeated state was in the hands of a harsh enemy; bands of guerillas – and quarantine laws – had to be faced in the North, and no one seemed anxious to buy cattle locally. It was hardly surprising that there were few trail drives in 1865. The cow hunts that seemed to occupy the time of every able-bodied man and boy in Texas in those bleak months seemed to be taking place more in hope than expectation.

Yet, in fact, the time was ripe for a cattle bonanza even before Joseph McCoy 'created' Abilene. An expanding, victorious North needed beef: what there was had gone to feed the armies, the settlers on the Minnesota-Iowa-Kansas frontier during the war having grown wheat. And the East was now in the grip of an ever-expanding industrial revolution in areas which had once been farmland, a revolution that war, as always in modern times, had accelerated. Also, the Frontier was heading westwards and railroads, given a giant push by the needs of war, were being built that would transport settlers by the

40: 'Stampede!' The dreaded word on any trail drive. Here Remington dramatically illustrates the danger the cowboy faced when running with and attempting to turn a stampeding herd.
COURTESY ROBIN MAY COLLECTION.

million. Work on the Union Pacific had been started in 1863, but it soon stopped, and only began in earnest, with the Central Pacific heading towards it from the West, following the close of the war. The two lines were to meet in Utah in 1869, and in just a decade an area roamed by the Indians and millions of buffalo was to become cattle country.

Back in 1865 and early 1866 Texas cowmen worked to get their herds branded and ready for the spring trails of 1866. It was a glorious period for young Texans and was to continue to be so. As was noted at the end of the last chapter, a Galveston newspaper of 1866 was lamenting that there was not a boy of American parentage learning a trade or reading for a profession west of the Colorado: they were learning to be cowboys. And meanwhile, their elders rounded up their own strayed stock, every maverick they could find, and any wild cattle they could catch.

1866 was to prove a grim year for those aiming at northern markets, though, as we shall see, a handful of cattlemen headed westwards with happier results. Not that the drovers who headed North were anything but optimistic at first. In these early days of the trail drives most cattle were driven by drovers (whose profession will be dealt with more fully later in this chapter). Having purchased Longhorns from the cattlemen at around five dollars a head and secured a crew, they headed northwards as did those cattlemen (ranchers) who drove their own herds. Their chief destination that year was the early cowtown of Baxter Springs, Kansas, near the border of Missouri and the Indian Territory, and if a sale was not effected there, the cattle would be driven to Sedalia, Missouri, to the Northeast, where they could be shipped on the Missouri Pacific Railroad. Some 250,000 Longhorns were on the move – and few were to find a market.

The troubles started near Baxter Springs – after expected difficulties from swollen rivers and Indians. The Indians were mainly members of the Five Civilised Tribes (Cherokees, Creeks, Choctaws, Chickasaws, Seminoles) who had been driven westwards on the unsavoury orders of President Andrew Jackson a generation earlier. We shall see what action they – and wilder Indians – took later, for in 1866 the whites were far more dangerous than any Indian.

Near Baxter Springs, armed gangs pretending to be worried about Texas fever were waiting to pounce, many of them veterans of pre-war Border butchery and wartime guerilla savagery. Herds were stolen, drovers and cowboys killed. As Joseph McCoy later put it; 'When, by outraging and robbing and, if needs be, by murdering the unfortunate drover, they became possessed of his stock, all fear of disease subsided.' Others made no pretence of combating the threat of disease, and killed and stole without alleged medical motive. If the trail herders were able to resist too effectively, the cattle could usually be stampeded. Sometimes desperadoes could be bought

41: A fatal step into a gopher hole, and rider and pony were thrown into the path of the maddened herd. Sometimes the cattle swept around them; but most times horse and rider were unrecognisable when found later.
COURTESY ROBIN MAY COLLECTION.

off, which was hardly satisfactory. Of course, some of the opposition to the Texans was genuine, from farmers who truly feared the fever; but it is hard to believe that they were more than a minority. The running was being made by men who had tormented the area for more than a decade, Kansas Jayhawkers and Border Ruffians from Missouri, and their lethal brothers in crime.

The best-known stories of the 1866 trails sum up the miseries of the year. George C. Duffield, who kept a diary, started out with a thousand steers in April and ended his journey with a few hundred in late October, but at least he was not subjected to the nightmare that sixteen-year-old Jim Daugherty endured.

He set out with five hands and some five hundred steers in the spring of 1866 and crossed the Red River intending to reach Sedalia via Baxter Springs and ship them to St Louis by rail.

Daugherty rode ahead to Baxter Springs, where he heard how another drover had been killed by outlaws after his herd had been stampeded. So he stopped his herd on the south side of the Kansas line and rode to Fort Scott, where he arranged to sell his stock to one Ben Keys. Then he went back and rejoined his herd, trailing them northwards along the Kansas-Missouri border. The small group of herders were on the alert, but they were jumped by some fifteen to twenty Jayhawkers, who ordered them to stop, meanwhile yelling at the herd. John Dobbins, riding point, started to draw his pistol, but was shot dead, while the terrified Longhorns stampeded.

42: His friends buried what was left of him after a cowboy was trampled to death during a stampede. This photograph of a cowboy funeral was made in 1892, but could well represent a similar scene at any time.
COURTESY KANSAS STATE HISTORICAL SOCIETY.

The gang disarmed Daugherty and led him to Cow Creek, where he was tied to a tree and whipped with hickory switches. Then they conferred on what to do with him. They agreed that he must be driving diseased cattle without bothering to check, but could not decide whether to hang him or whip him to death; but, fortunately, one of the Jayhawkers was softened by Daugherty's youth and talked the rest into letting him go.

To his delight he found only about 150 of his cattle had been lost or stolen, his men having rounded up the rest. They buried

John Dobbins, then headed south to plan their next move. The upshot was that Daugherty returned to Fort Scott and told Ben Keys about the attack on him. Keys at once got him a guide who led the herd by night through thinly populated country to Fort Scott, where the determined youth was able to sell his stock at a profit.

Most drovers, even those who escaped whippings, were less lucky that dismal year. One former Missourian, W. H. Farmer, was allowed into the state because of friends, but too many endured attacks, deliberate stampedes and equally deliberate slaughter of their herds to make the thought of trail drives in 1867 anything but a grim one. And a number of drovers and their men were killed. Some tried wintering in Indian Territory or in southern Kansas or Missouri, but a combination of drought, prairie fires and a series of blizzards devalued their stock so much that no one wanted to buy it.

43: Lightning, a sudden noise, or other distraction could start a stampede. Another woodcut from McCoy's *Historic Sketches*.
COURTESY ROBIN MAY COLLECTION.

1867, the year of salvation, dawned bleakly enough and soon Colorado, Missouri, Kansas, Nebraska, Illinois and Kentucky had all passed measures to keep the tick-bearing Longhorns out. The laws varied, but all either barred or restricted the cattle, the only loophole being in Kansas where a corridor south and west of McPherson, then the furthest outpost of settlement, was left open. And drovers were to be allowed to head a little further north to ship their cattle on the Union Pacific Railway Eastern Division (renamed the Kansas Pacific in 1869) which was then heading westwards. Tight regulations included guarantees of payment for damage to Kansas stock, avoiding public highways, and keeping five miles from any settler unless he gave written consent. It was hardly enough for Texans to declare a state holiday, but it was a glimmer of hope.

But how could they expect anyone to have a shipping point big enough and in the right place for the 1867 season? They did not yet know about Joseph Geiting McCoy.

Before meeting McCoy, other 1866 events must be chronicled, the first being the blazing of the Goodnight-Loving Trail. The pair whose names it bore met that year. Oliver Loving, who had trailed herds to Illinois and Colorado before the war, was fifty-four years of age and Charles Goodnight was thirty. Loving had only a year to live, for in 1867 he was jumped by Comanches and wounded in the arm and side. He escaped and reached Fort Sumner, New Mexico, to die of infection, as the local doctor 'had never amputated any limbs and did not want to undertake such work.'

44: Charles Goodnight, whose part in establishing the Goodnight-Loving trail, places him among the giants of the cattlemens' West. When he died he owned an estimated 20 million acres of Texas rangeland.
COURTESY OF THE ROSE COLLECTION, WESTERN HISTORY COLLECTIONS, UNIVERSITY OF OKLAHOMA LIBRARY.

Charlie Goodnight was more fortunate, graduating from mere cattleman/cowman to become the archetypal cattle baron (who, unlike some, knew everything there was to know about all aspects of the business). He even fathered the chuck wagon. A cowboy almost from infancy, he served in the Texas Rangers during the Civil War, fighting off Comanches and Kiowas on the Frontier. After the war, unlike the majority of cattlemen who looked northwards, he set his sights on New Mexico, where Navahos on the Bosque Redondo Reservation needed feeding, as did the soldiers guarding them and fighting the Apaches there and in Arizona.

The Indian barrier was formidable, but by striking westwards across the Staked Plains it might be possible to avoid it – and after New Mexico the mining country to the north in Colorado was beckoning. The snag was a grim eighty-mile stretch in Texas from the Middle Concho to the Horsehead crossing on the Pecos River, a region totally waterless except for very occasional and unpredictable rainfalls. Goodnight had a high regard for the tough Longhorns, but until he had the good fortune to fall in with Oliver Loving, he could not find anyone else to share his vision.

The pair became partners, merging their herds in June and setting out with two thousand cattle and eighteen men – and the prototype chuck wagon, a rebuilt Army wagon, big and durable, complete with a water barrel on each side, a canvas covering and – the unique feature – the chuck box with its hinged lid like a desk, and its desk-like drawers and cubbyholes. It was drawn by oxen.

The herd was a mixed one of steers, cows and bulls, which made for problems, as calves appeared. Goodnight had planned to carry them in the chuck wagon until they gained strength, but the idea was a failure and they had to be killed to his bitter regret. He was never to take a mixed herd again on this route.

The eighty-mile stretch proved as grim as expected and for three days and nights Goodnight got no sleep as he rode at point and on the flanks encouraging men and beasts. By the third night the cattle were in a ghastly state and the men were little better. But there could be no stopping or the herd would never have risen again. The men strove to keep the leaders in

45: The resumption of the drives and the movement of cattle out of Texas and Kansas after the Civil War created many problems, among them attacks by ex-guerrillas and 'Jayhawkers'. Some claimed they attacked the Texans for fear of Texas fever. Others used it as an excuse to beat or whip young cowboys before releasing them on payment of a toll or part of the herd. Occasionally the whole herd was stolen and men killed. Fortunately, when the Chisholm and other trails bypassed domesticated areas such attacks grew less.
COURTESY ROBIN MAY COLELCTION.

control so that the drag, with Loving in charge, would not be left behind but, when the cattle smelt water at 2am, Goodnight let those that could run towards it. At the Pecos there was chaos, with the first to reach it being pushed right across by those behind before they could drink. Others were trampled, bogged in quicksand or drowned, so that to the hundred whose carcases lay strewn along the trail were added another hundred victims. Yet Goodnight and Loving had triumphed, crossing the seemingly impassable and with a mixed herd. After a rest, they reached Fort Sumner where they were paid eight cents a pound for every steer. While Oliver Loving headed northwards to Colorado, there to sell the cows, bulls and calves to cattleman John Wesley Iliff, Charlie Goodnight headed back to Texas with a mule carrying $12,000 in gold. It was a triumph indeed.

Back in Texas Goodnight collected another herd, his gold allowing him to pick his steers. He only lost five of them on the way back to New Mexico. Another newcomer to New Mexico that year was John S. Chisum, destined to be as famous as Goodnight himself. It was cruel of fate to allow Loving, older than either of them, to miss the fruits of his triumph.

There was one other epic drive that year, a drive that had been heading for Kansas only to be received in the traditional manner of 1866. The cattleman in charge was Ohio-born Nelson Story who was not content with striking it rich in the goldfields of Montana but decided to put his money into Longhorns, a thousand of them. Being stopped at Baxter Springs, he decided to gamble on a long drive to the mines of Montana, his old stamping ground. He set off along the Oregon Trail route with a combined wagon train and trail herd, heading straight into country full of hostile Sioux. For Red Cloud's War was just beginning, triggered off by the decision to build forts to protect the Bozeman Trail through the Powder River country to the Montana mines. The Military had little sympathy with Story's plan, but with his twenty-seven men armed with Remington breech-loaders at a time when the Indians were mainly relying on bows and arrows, he took no notice. They reached Virginia City, Montana, on 9 December, the first and last trail herd to go up the Powder River Valley for four years. The worst incident had occurred near Fort Reno when the Sioux had wounded two cowboys and run off part of the herd. One of Story's men recalled the incident later when asked how many cattle they had lost.

'Not a single head. We just followed those Indians into the Bad Lands and got the cattle back.'

'Did they yield the steers willingly?'

'Well, you might say so. We surprised them in their camp and they weren't in shape to protest much against our taking back the cattle.'

46: Red Cloud, chief of the Oglala Sioux, whose warriors kept cattlemen out of Wyoming's Powder River country in the late 1860s.

COURTESY THE NATIONAL ARCHIVES, WASHINGTON, D.C.

Joseph G. McCoy was twenty-nine when he had his great idea and his career, character and abilities made him the man to carry that idea through to fruition. Born on an Illinois farm, he was far more than a cattle dealer, which is the usual description of him as he was in 1867, for he knew the whole livestock market – mules, cattle, hogs, sheep – knew it as a farmer as well as a shipper. And while the railroad bosses of Chicago and St Louis seemed blissfully unaware of the potentialities of the cattle trade, McCoy, currently a partner with his brothers in a cattle shipping firm, was pursuing, as he put it, 'a waking thought, a sleeping dream'.

47: A rarely published photograph of Joseph G. McCoy from a family portrait circa 1870.
COURTESY MARGOT MCCOY GAYLE AND STEWART P. VERCKLER.

It was a dream worth dreaming, a dream that was to be the salvation of the Texas cattle industry, was to make Chicago the headquarters of the beef industry, and the nation as a whole give its allegiance to beef rather than pork.

The vital factor was the location of his proposed shipping point. McCoy's fertile imagination was inflamed by a younger man, Charles Gross, who had visited Texas just after the Civil War. He told his fellow Illinoisan of the vast number of cattle and horses running wild, until soon McCoy was excitedly making plans. And another Illinois man, W. W. Sugg, told McCoy of his sufferings on the trail at the hands of Jayhawkers, who were as prepared to maltreat a Northerner driving cattle northwards as they were Texans. So McCoy conceived his plan, which he put in his own rather heavy prose in his *Historic Sketches of the Cattle Trade of the West and Southwest* (1874):

> This young man [McCoy himself] conceived the idea of opening up an outlet for Texan cattle. Being impressed with a knowledge of the number of cattle in Texas and the difficulties of getting them to market by the routes and means then in use, and realizing the great disparity of Texas values and Northern prices of cattle, he set himself to thinking and studying to hit upon some plan whereby these great extremes could be equalized. The plan (finally decided upon) was to establish at some accessible point a depot or market to which a Texan drover could bring his stock unmolested, and there, failing to find a better buyer, he could go upon the public highways to any market in the country he wished. In short, it was to establish a market whereat the Southern drover and the Northern buyer would meet upon an equal footing, and both be undisturbed by mobs or swindling thieves.

Easier said than done, but McCoy started looking and, finally, after several disappointments, lighted on a tiny village called Abilene, which then consisted of a dozen or so log cabins, a few slightly grander business buildings and a flourishing prairie dog colony. But it was on the railroad, though as yet there was no passenger station, just a post to mark where trains should stop, with a hook on it for mail.

Ironically, Abilene was within the banned zone for cattle, but there were so few settlers in the area that no one tried to enforce the law. It was an ideal spot because of the lack of settlers and abundance of water and good grass.

The speed with which McCoy went to work was phenomenal. It was mid-June, 1867 when he selected Abilene; by the 18th he had bought 250 acres of land to start his cattle yards; and he began building them by the beginning of July with wood that had to be transported to the site, Abilene being treeless. By 1 September, he had a shipping yard that could hold a thousand cattle, also an office and a barn, while his soon-to-be-famous Drovers' Cottage, three storeys high and with a livery stable behind it, was being erected. He was also building a bank.

Meanwhile, he softened up local opposition, enlisted the crucially important support of the governor of Kansas, hired Gross as his accountant, and had sent handbills to Texas which sang the praises of Abilene as a shipping centre. These were followed by W. W. Sugg, whose job it was to find drovers who were hoping for a market. And the drovers he found liked what they heard.

Sugg's mission was to promote autumn drives, but near Abilene there were already cattle waiting for the stockyards to open, one of which was able to load a forty-car train in two hours. Fearful or angry settlers, and many who were both, were talked to by McCoy so successfully that they stopped being hostile and were further persuaded when Texas drovers at the meeting offered large sums for vegetables and hay. As for McCoy, though some settlers were still suspicious of him,

48: Col. O. W. Wheeler's first herd en route to Abilene in 1867, from a woodcut published in the Kansas Pacific Railway's 'Guide Map' and McCoy's *Historic. Sketches of the Cattle Trade of the West and Southwest.* **The artist depicts the cattle like an army on the march, whereas in fact they would have been spread out over a much greater distance.**
COURTESY ROBIN MAY COLLECTION.

49: Black Beaver, a Delaware Indian who became one of the greatest guides in the pre-Civil War West, from a plate made by an unknown photographer and copied in 1869 by A. Z. Shindler of Washington.
COURTESY SMITHSONIAN INSTITUTION.

townspeople and Texans admired him and his soaring imagination and liked him as a man.

Inevitably, there could not be a beef bonanza at Abilene in 1867, but a significant start was made. The very first cattle to arrive had come up the Shawnee Trail and been sold in Indian Territory before reaching Abilene. The first herd direct from Texas was 2,400 strong and led by a Californian, Colonel O. W. Wheeler, who with fifty-four cowboys armed with Colt six-shooters and sixteen-shot Henry repeating rifles, had headed north from San Antonio. His destination had been the Pacific Coast, but after his journey up the as-yet-unnamed new trail, he sold out in Abilene. With such a high-powered outfit, he had had no trouble with Indians, and he was to lead other herds up the trail in later years.

The first shipment out of Abilene was on 5 September, with twenty cars Chicago-bound. As the hotel was not yet ready, McCoy and his friends toasted each other in a tent. Though only around 35,000 cattle came up the trail in 1867, McCoy had no doubts that the future was bright.

It helped that he had a flair for publicity, describing the new trail to potential users in glowing terms: 'It is more direct, it has more prairie, less timber, more small streams and fewer large ones, altogether better grass and fewer flies, no civilized Indian tax or wild Indian disturbances, than any other route yet driven.'

This apparent paradise on the Plains was to become the

50: Jesse Chisholm, whose trail bore his name and immortalised it. From a tintype believed to have been made by E. E. Henry of Leavenworth, Kansas.
COURTESY THE KANSAS STATE HISTORICAL SOCIETY.

immortal Chisholm Trail. It was some 150 miles west of the Shawnee Trail and, as the endpaper map shows, it virtually went straight through the centre of Indian Territory. Buffalo, Indians and the occasional white trader used the trail before it was blazed by a number of military units, the first being six companies of dragoons in 1855. The first large body was led by Colonel William H. Emory who headed north in 1861. It was guided by Delaware scouts under the renowned plainsman, Black Beaver, who showed the way for 750 soldiers and 150 women and children and noncombatants. They were bound for Fort Leavenworth, and Indians loyal to the North used the same line of retreat.

Among the Indian refugees was Jesse Chisholm, who was living with the Wichitas. He was an old trader from Tennessee, whose father was of Scots descent and whose mother was a Cherokee. Indians and whites trusted him and he was used as a scout, when he was not trading. The trail south from his trading post on the North Canadian began to be called the Chisholm, though it was not until a few years after his death in 1868 in his late sixties that the trail as a whole became known as the Chisholm Trail, the first apparent newspaper reference to it by name being on 18 May 1870. Other names for the Trail included the Abilene Trail, the Great Cattle Trail, and McCoy's Trail or Extension, and sometimes just the Cattle Trail, but by 1874 a Texas newspaper could call it the 'famous Chisholm Trail'. So it was that Jesse Chisholm, whose aunt had been one of Sam Houston's wives, became a Frontier immortal almost by accident. The Trail and its rivals are described in more detail in Appendix I.

Other Kansas towns wanted their share of the action in 1868 and sent slick talkers south, so W. W. Sugg was rushed down to counteract their claims and tell the drovers the truth – that buyers awaited them in Abilene. Although some cattle were driven to Junction City, the place was never a rival, and Wichita, where the Chisholm Trail ended, had to watch helplessly as the Longhorns passed on to Abilene, because until 1872 the place lacked a railroad. So Abilene's reign as the premier cowtown was to continue until the end of the 1871 season. But 1868 was to be the first boom year, not least because McCoy advertised so widely in Texas and among northern cattlemen. When the herds started to arrive in the summer of '68, there were indeed plenty of buyers awaiting them at the now-completed Drover's Cottage. McCoy had even had his route straightened and shortened a little and marked portions of it with piles of sod. He was never one to leave anything to chance.

51: Settlers on the cattle trails lived in homes similar to this one photographed in Custer County, Nebraska, in 1889 or 1890, and they were in constant fear of the cattlemen, though they were rarely molested.
COURTESY THE SOLOMON D. BUTCHER COLLECTION, NEBRASKA STATE HISTORICAL SOCIETY.

Cattle started arriving in April and a thousand carloads of steers had been shipped out by the end of June. There were not enough stock cars available, so some flatcars were given frameworks to convert them into cattlecars. Meanwhile, McCoy held public auctions and actually sent a wild-west show into Illinois and Missouri, 'feeder' country where beeves were fattened before marketing. The combination of buffaloes, wild horses and skilled horsemen, though it lost money, was a splendid advertisement, and that year 75,000 Longhorns reached Abilene. McCoy despatched more than 45,000 of them East by rail, while the rest were trailed northwards and were to lay the foundations of new ranges in Montana and Wyoming.

So the year was a great success, though it would have been even greater if Texas fever had not hit Kansas and, particularly, Illinois. As for 1869, it was even more of a boom year, with twelve-dollar steers fetching thirty dollars at the railhead. The grass was so nutritious that year that the Longhorns fattened en route. But even in good years, coming up the Chisholm Trail was always a major operation and often a perilous one . . .

The average number of Longhorns in a trail herd was between one and two thousand, with some six to a dozen cowboys in charge of them. The usual wage was $30 a month, with top

52: The chuckwagon and the cook making pies. Perhaps the man seated in front of it and grinning is doing so because he believes he will be the first in line when the cook yells: 'Come and get it!'
COURTESY NEBRASKA STATE HISTORICAL SOCIETY.

hands drawing $40, and all were entitled to a month's wages at the trail's end to get them back to Texas. Every man had from two to four horses and would change mounts several times each day to save wearing them out, and at the end of the drive most of the horses were sold. In the early years the herds going up the Chisholm Trail were usually led by drovers, though, later, big ranches usually drove their own cattle, hiring a trail boss – also known as a boss herder – for the drive. And in the early days some northern cattlemen went to Texas to drive herds back to their ranges.

The drover made contracts with ranchers for the number of Longhorns he wanted to drive to market. He then selected his cowboys with the utmost care, also hiring a wrangler to look after the horses. He bought a chuck wagon, an important feature of which, not so far mentioned, might be a 'caboose' which hung below it, made of cowhide and ready to receive every scrap of wood that could be found to throw in it against the time the trail ran through timberless country. The wood was also used when the going was wet. The cook – also hired by the drover – was an even more important figure on the long trail than on the range.

All the drover's Longhorns were given a special road brand for the trip in addition to their original owners' markings. Naturally, the drover obtained a bill of sale from each of his customers, otherwise he was liable to be accused of theft later on. It was no mean bill, for it contained brands, earmarks and other signs of identification. As Everett Dick has written; 'The appearance of a bill of sale was akin to an Egyptian tablet covered with hieroglyphics.'

When a rancher was himself sending his cattle north, he hired a trail boss, gave him his orders and enough money, then said: 'I'll see you in Abilene!' or wherever. If he was a cattle king, with many thousands of Longhorns to despatch, he did not send them all at once, but divided them into herds of around 2,500 each. Ranchers travelled northwards by rail or boat and were there waiting for their herds' arrival, or sometimes they would go some way down the trail to link up with them. As for drovers, they sometimes made several trips a season.

The vastness of Texas affected the time of starting up the trail, but March and April seem to have been the usual months. An early start ensured good pasture along the trail and many cattle were allowed to graze on the northern grass to build

53: Whips or quirts, as the cowboys called them, are rarely seen in Western films but were a useful and necessary aid on a trail drive.
COURTESY ROBIN MAY COLLECTION.

them up again after the long march before selling them.

Herds consisting solely of steers – usually four or five year olds – and also mixed herds went up the trail. As we have seen on the Goodnight-Loving Trail, the mixed herds created problems, besides which steers walked more steadily than cows. However, steers were more prone to stampede.

An experienced trail boss or drover never tried to force a herd, aiming, after the Longhorns were 'trail broke', at around ten or twelve miles a day. The first few days out, however, found the drover – in charge, after all, of cattle from different ranches – keeping up a faster pace, partly to get them away from 'home', partly to tire them out so that they would settle down at night. Early stampedes by cattle wanting to get back to their usual feeding places had to be avoided. Meanwhile, the art was to make the cattle think they were dictating the pace, not the cowboys: the Longhorns kept fatter that way.

Fort Worth, Texas, was a key supply base on the trail, for food had to be bought for at least a month, there being no stores between there and Kansas in the early days. Flour, bacon and coffee were the basics. When Baylis John Fletcher, author of *Up the Trail in '79*, as noted earlier, was in Fort Worth with a herd bossed by George Arnett, the drummers (salesmen) descended on the outfit eager to see the boss. By previous arrangement, the oldest cowboy of the outfit, Steve 'Shug' Pointer, was taken by the drummers to be the boss and gratefully accepted 'a box of fine cigars, some whisky, and other blandishments'. When he had been plied with enough gifts, one

54: A bearded cowboy quirts his horse into a gallop during a roundup of bronchos or a ranch remuda, from a drawing by Remington.

COURTESY ROBIN MAY COLLECTION.

of the boys rode up and yelled at him: 'Shug, the boss says come on, you lazy cuss, and get to work, or he'll turn you off at Fort Worth.' A cowboy yell rent the air to celebrate a rare success in turning the tables on a slick salesman, though Shug would have liked the game kept up a little longer. However, as the boss later bought two months supplies, the drummers went away happy.

A boss posted his best trail hands as pointers, leading the herd. Alongside the herd rose swing men, then flank men and, lastly, the drag men/tail riders/trailers, condemned to 'eat dust' and to look after the 'drags' – the weaklings, the slowcoaches and the plain dumb. Fortunately, the job went in rotation. The drags had to be kept moving for they set the pace of the whole and, as they always arrived late at water, their guardians had to get them upstream to prevent them having to drink muddied water.

As opposed to loafers, there were natural leaders, the most famous of all being Charles Goodnight's lead steer, Old Blue. No dumb critter he, his owner considered him worth a dozen extra hands. The canny Longhorn went up trail after trail and became something of a snob, refusing to mix with the common herd. He preferred the saddle herd or, better still, the chuck wagon, where he expected the cook to feed him.

The boss, who rode ahead scouting for pasture and water, would stop his herd around 11am and let them graze while the men had their meal. If Cookie had reached the spot in advance, they might get a newly cooked meal, if not, they would eat food he had prepared for them while he was cooking breakfast. The afternoon drive, with the Longhorns keen to quench their thirst, tended to be easier going. The cowboys tightened up the herd in the late afternoon and aimed to reach the camp the boss had found them before dusk. They hoped to bed the steers high and dry and not too near woods that might contain Indians or wild animals, and naturally avoided ravines into which the cattle might plunge in a stampede.

55: The trail herd flankers.
COURTESY THE ERWIN E. SMITH COLLECTION OF RANGE LIFE PHOTOGRAPHS, LIBRARY OF CONGRESS.

Now the herd was in a circle. The animals had nibbled their way along the trail but were ready for more grass, while the cowboys took it in turn to have their main meal of the day, their supper. By now they had made the circle more compact and their charges were beginning to settle down for the night. The last to settle and first to rise were the hornless cattle whose lack of defences caused them to avoid the centre of the herd.

The cook's last job in strange country was to set his chuck wagon's tongue with the North Star, which acted as a compass for the herd. There were always two men on night guard, relief coming at regular intervals of two hours or longer. They would comfort a restless herd with humming or soft singing and were expected to sing even in a storm, for it was vital for the cattle to hear a human voice. Too bad if a man couldn't hold a tune, he still had to make some soothing noise. And, of course, singing helped to keep a tired herder awake.

Around midnight, the Longhorns used to get up, stretch themselves and yawn, then settle down for some more sleep. The hands usually turned in early after a long day and because of the likelihood of broken nights, guard duty apart. They might strip to their underclothes in hot weather, but more often they would only take off boots and belts. They either slept with their reigns in their hand or with their night horse picketed nearby. Even when things were going well, a long night's sleep was out of the question. Big outfits had a 'nighthawk' to take care of the *remuda* at night, which lessened the strain on the wrangler. Youngster he might be (though a few outfits used old hands good for little else), but his responsibilities were non-stop and included looking for any horse that went missing. And, as if looking after the horse herd were not enough, he had to find wood for the fire and help Cookie wash the dishes. Yet the bright wrangler on a trail herd would be instructed as well as teased by the cowpunchers, and, as noted, be getting fine grounding for the life of a cowboy. ('Cowpuncher'? This now widely used word was not in general use until the '80s. It was

56: A moment of relaxation on the drive, cowboys around a chuckwagon.
COURTESY PANHANDLE-PLAINS HISTORICAL MUSEUM.

derived from the metal-pointed prod 'punchers' used to force cattle into stock cars.)

Whatever movies suggest, there was rarely much trouble among the cowboys on a trail. With drink banned, and with no camp-followers except – very occasionally – an owner's wife, two major causes of friction were absent. (For a remarkable lady on the trail, see page 74.) The trail boss was not a man to be lightly crossed, and nor was the cook, his second-in-command. Very occasionally there was a gunfight, but the worst recorded incident was a freakish piece of horror. A Mexican trail hand, acting as cook, went berserk one May night in 1873 in Cooke County, Texas. Wielding an axe, he chopped off the heads of four sleeping cowboys and was just about to do the same to a fifth when his intended victim woke up and roared out in alarm. The maniac escaped. But, generally, there were troubles enough on the trail from outside causes which kept even potential troublemakers occupied.

The hardships of the trail included thieves, Indians and angry settlers, also floods, swollen rivers, storms, prairie fires, stampedes and falls. With such a list no wonder that Teddy Blue, as mentioned earlier, recalled lack of sleep as being the worst hardship of all. No wonder that young healthy men reached the cowtowns run down and exhausted and liable to go wild. And they were young. Very few except the boss and the cook were as old as thirty.

57: Samuel Maverick, a cattleman on the San Antònio River, who neglected to brand his calves, and lost them to greedy neighbours, and whose name lives on to denote 'maverick' or unbranded cattle.
COURTESY ROBIN MAY COLLECTION.

58: Wolf Robe, a Southern Cheyenne. The Cheyennes were among the most warlike tribes on the Plains, as many cowboys discovered to their cost. This old warrior was photographed in 1909.
COURTESY THE SMITHSONIAN INSTITUTION.

There were few occasions when danger was banished. A rattler could join a sleeping cowboy and not take kindly to sudden movement or it could strike his horse's leg. A prairie-dog could bring him crashing down, while cholera put some cowboys under the ground.

Even if there was no resulting stampede, storms could be hellish affairs on the open prairie. Cowboys were knocked from their horses by lightning and many were killed or badly burned by it. It was hardly surprising that many of them were terrified of it – and let it be remembered that they could never take shelter: their duty was towards their cattle. An 1882 storm killed fourteen steers, six or seven horses and two men on the trail, and there was at least one cowboy who threw away his pistol in case it attracted lightning. One tough Texan trail boss was not scared but angered by lightning. At the height of a storm he took off his hat and roared at the Almighty: 'All right, you old bald-headed son of a bitch up there, if you want to kill me, come on do it!' The Almighty had no such intention.

Rustlers were not a major hazard to trail herds heading northwards in Texas as the Texas Rangers were notably good at tracking down cattle thieves, but they managed to stampede and steal stock on a number of occasions. It was up to the herdsmen to handle the situation themselves, however, especially in Indian Territory where there were no peace officers in the early days, just a scattering of soldiers who did not see the protection of trail herds as part of their job. As for Kansas lawmen, even

58.

supposing that they were willing to act for the drovers, they could not guarantee to be able to raise posses, though it was known to happen.

Quarrels with Kansas farmers were constant irritants and many settlers claimed damages against the Texas outfits, most being settled out of court for anything from half a dollar to two hundred. And more money was on the way for the 'nesters' in the shape of cow dung, the 'chips' that made fine winter fuel.

More serious were Indian predators, Comanches, Cheyennes, Osages, Kiowas and others, until the destruction of the great buffalo herds and action by the military tamed most of them by the mid-'70s. In terms of actual danger, cattle trails to the Far West were more hazardous than the Chisholm, where the main troubles were begging and stealing. But there were some alarming encounters. Four hundred Comanches blocked the progress of an outfit herding a thousand steers in 1869 and laid on an impressive display of horsemanship for the vastly outnumbered cowboys. As they sped by, the young braves – standing on, lying on and holding on to the sides of their ponies – killed twenty five steers with arrows. They then enjoyed a feast of raw flesh before letting the cowpunchers head up the trail again. A year later in Kansas, Cheyennes ran off with R. R. Savage's entire herd, worth $18,000.

When the army gradually gained control, Indians tended half to beg and half to demand steers and were usually given one or more poor quality beasts if they would not be satisfied with a sash or a bandanna. Horses could still disappear, however, one 'friendly' tribe running off some in the night and bringing them back next day for a reward.

One of the best cowboys versus Indians stories is related by Edward Everett Dale in his *Cow Country*. A Kiowa chief demanded six beeves of a trail boss but was told he could only have two. That was not enough for the chief, who announced that he would come with his braves that night and stampede the herd. The boss said that the chief should be sure to bring a spade and was asked why.

'Well,' said the boss, 'the cook broke the handle of our spade yesterday. When you come to stampede the cattle, I aim to kill you. Unless you bring a spade, we can't bury you.'

The chief went away with two beeves.

A rare example of ruthless action by a cowboy is related in John Wesley Hardin's autobiography, the ruthlessness, needless to say, being shown by himself. The killer was going up the Chisholm with a herd and was near the Kansas line. According to him, while he had been away from camp a band of Osages had frightened the cook and hands almost to death and had stolen a fancy silver bridle of his. As the Osages had been cutting out little bunches of cattle from the herd some days previously, Hardin had told the hands to shoot the first Osage that cut another cow. Now, with his silver bridle gone, he was feeling angry:

59: Apache warriors circa the mid 1870s. Cattlemen were not freed from the menace of these ferocious guerrilla fighters until the mid 1880s.

COURTESY THE OFFICE OF THE CHIEF OF ENGINEERS.

In a little while about twenty bucks came to the herd, rode in, and commenced to cut out cattle. I rode up to where they were and saw a big Indian using my fancy silver bridle. I asked him how much he would take for it and offered him $5. He grunted an assent and gave me the bridle. When I got it, I told him that was my bridle and someone had stolen it from camp that morning. He frowned and grunted and started to get the bridle back, trying to pull it off my horse. I 'jabbed' him with my pistol, and when this would not stop him, I struck him over the head with it. He fell back and yelled to his companions. This put the devil in them. They came up in a body and demanded cattle again. I told them 'no' as I had done before. An Indian rode to the herd and cut out a big beef steer. I told him to get out of the herd and pulled my pistol to emphasize my remarks. He was armed and drew his, saying that if I did not let him cut the beef out, he would kill the animal. I told him that if he killed the animal, I would kill him. Well, he killed the beef and I killed him. The other Indians promptly vanished. If they hadn't, there would have been more dead Indians around that herd. The beef he had killed lay dead on the trail, so I mounted him by tying the dead Indian on his back and drove on.

Some herds were still being driven up the old Shawnee Trail to Baxter Springs and were sometimes grazed on Cherokee lands. In December 1867, the Cherokees levied a toll of ten cents a head and the other local tribes affected followed suit, the Creeks demanding twenty seven and a half cents a head. These 'taxes' were an additional reason for the demise of the Shawnee Trail.

A milder human hazard was the inspector, who looked over a

60: Quanah Parker, the greatest Comanche war chief – whose mother was white. The Comanches were a constant threat to cattle drives herding westwards until the mid-1870s.

COURTESY THE SMITHSONIAN INSTITUTION.

herd to check that the drover or boss was the true owner. All that was needed was the strange-looking bill of sale mentioned earlier when the inspector appeared: a number of them were stationed at the crossings on the Red River, and their activities could delay herds for several days, which did not add to their popularity. But it was endured in Texas except when bogus inspectors tried to levy a fee. And, outside Texas, drovers resented anyone trying to check their credentials in the name of authority.

The two most dangerous hazards of the trail were river crossings and stampedes. The crossings were often so formidable that they gave birth to the tribute, 'A man to ride the river with'. There were no bridges or ferryboats in the trailing days except a few of the former over small streams. In dry weather these could usually be forded with ease, though the bigger ones had to be crossed by swimming, and in rainy seasons rivers were swollen enough for cowboys to call what they had to do 'big swimming'. Drives in the Spring and Fall often coincided with floods and there were years when every river from the Red to the Arkansas invited 'big swimming'. Drownings of cattle and horses were all too common, and cowboys perished as well, while some streams had quicksands which also claimed horses and cows as victims. Sometimes men as well as their mounts had to be rescued by rope.

It was the boss's job to find an area of solid footing on both banks of a stream and on its bottom. His men changed to their best 'swimmin' hosses' while he made sure that the time of day was right: he tried to ensure that the Longhorns would not swim directly into the glare of the sinking sun.

The boss started his cattle crossing upstream of the spot where he wanted them ashore on the far bank, as they would drift with the river's current. Steers would sometimes fight shy of starting into the water and needed urging. Crossings were done en masse or in groups of around thirty cattle, the cowboys taking up positions similar to those on the trail to encourage the animals across. Sometimes they needed no urging and, as one herder recalled, swam 'proud as swans', calves included. They made an unforgettable sight. But things often went wrong. A strange sound, a floating log, a sudden eddy and the leading steers might turn and the whole herd would soon be circling wildly in the water.

61: Most of the cowboys on the trail looked upon water as a means of appeasing their own or their horses and cattle's thirsts, so it was rare to find time or the opportunity to 'get wet all over and mean it'.
COURTESY THE KANSAS STATE HISTORICAL SOCIETY.

Into the terrified throng the cowboys had to ride, shouting at the cattle, flailing at them and risking their lives trying to get them heading once more for the far bank. Inevitably, some hands were flung into the water, when it became a case of swimming, weighed down by heavy boots, or grabbing the tail of a Longhorn or a horse and getting pulled to the north bank. There was one occasion when more than a hundred cattle drowned -- in the North Canadian in 1869 – and cowboys, too, perished.

Charlie Siringo recalled a crossing of the Salt Fork of the Arkansas when the lead steers balked in mid-stream from a combination of flotsam, fast water and the drowning of a point rider's horse. Most of the herd got back to the south bank, but the cowboys were forced to remain there a week, most of the time in pouring rain, until the river became low enough for a safe crossing.

Getting the chuck wagon across was a more mundane task than urging the herd through the water, but it was hard work. Normally, the oxen or mules were taken from the cart or wagon and swam the stream. Then a rope – made of several tied picket ropes – was fixed to the wagon and it was dragged across. The chuck box's contents went over by raft. Occasionally, pontoons were fastened to the wagon which was then floated across.

The menace of quicksands was very real, making even drying-up rivers potential death traps. The quicksand bottom of the South Canadian had mires that 'would bog a saddle blanket', wrote cowpuncher Andy Adams. It needed four of the chuck wagon mules to rescue a steer from its lethal grasp.

For the cowboys, the Red River was more than just another stream to be crossed; indeed, it was often low enough to be waded. But this was where they and their herds left Texas and

62: A typical rope corral with the horse remuda.
COURTESY PANHANDLE-PLAINS HISTORICAL MUSEUM.

ventured into Indian Territory. A boss would get rid of poor hands at Red River Station and hire himself replacements. Then it was time to cross – except in a year like 1871 when the river was so high from the spring thaw that 60,000 Longhorns were queuing on the south bank, waiting for a chance to swim over. And in better times there were its quicksands. The Red River was a symbol of the trail herding era and it is fitting that the best of all films about a trail drive (for all its human melodrama) is called *Red River*.

But if river crossings on the journey North were so often fraught with tension and danger, stampedes were always the most fearful hazards of all.

A single startled Longhorn could set off a stampede. The wild rush usually happened at night, especially in rainy seasons and during storms. A sudden flash of lightning, a thunderclap, a howl of a coyote, a horse's neigh, the striking of a match, a sneeze . . . sometimes a herd started running for no apparent reason at all.

A single steer, nervous or difficult or both, could cause a number of stampedes and, when detected for certain, had to be shot or – as William Hoover did in Kansas in 1869 – given to a Choctaw Indian for two yearlings.

Electric storms were particularly tense times, but at least the hands were alerted. Their charges heard the distant thunder, then, with the storm drawing near, the tips of the cattle's horns glowed with balls of phosphorescent light, a grim omen of trouble to come. The night guards sang to the cattle to try and soothe them, but by now the first of them were starting to stand. Then the storm began and so did the stampede.

The earth trembled under the clatter of hoofs, horns clanged and a great heat was generated, as Charlie Goodnight recalled – 'The faces of the men riding on the leeward side of the herd would be almost blistered, as if they had been struck by a blast from a furnace', and the smell from the clashing horns and hoofs was almost overpowering.

Those hands not already mounted sprang into their saddles and galloped after the herd. They could not stop them, but tried to turn them into a huge circle. Using this 'milling' process, they gradually narrowed the circle, but did not let it become too solid for fear of harming the cattle in the centre. Gradually the frightened beasts calmed down, the cowboys singing to them, presumably hoarsely by this time. They had sung during the stampede, not to the cattle but to reassure the other hands that they were still there. If one was down, an attempt was made to stop the mill and clear the area where horse and rider had fallen. Their best chance was the fact that Longhorns tried to avoid obstacles.

It is often stated that cowboys fired their pistols into the ground near the stampeders' ears to make them turn, but Teddy Blue, a veteran of many stampedes,claimed this was all fiction and would have made the cattle run even faster. The only time he knew of it happening was to try and stop a herd running over a bank, but it only partially succeeded.

After the stampede there was always a danger of another – and another. One herd stampeded eighteen times in a single night. Some stampedes could be ended in four or five miles, but some went on for a week and covered hundreds of miles. Needless to say, the cattle were worth far less by the end of such a strenuous bout of exercise. And after a stampede, long or short, the herd was counted and hands set out to look for those that were missing.

Inevitably, many Longhorns were killed in stampedes, the most notorious loss being 2,700, who, despite frantic efforts by their punchers, crashed down into a ravine near the Brazos River in Texas in 1876.

An unknown, but probably not vast, number of cowboys

63: Cutting out a steer from the herd.

COURTESY THE ERWIN E. SMITH COLLECTION OF RANGE LIFE PHOTOGRAPHS, LIBRARY OF CONGRESS.

died in stampedes. Death could be very quick, but the aftermath was often horrifying for the dead man's friends. In one Nebraska tragedy the cowboys came across what was left of one of their comrades – the butt of a six-shooter.

There were some amazing escapes. One sleeping cowboy woke up to find Longhorns racing past him on each side, while he was being protected by his horse standing over him. Few cowboys were eager to test the advice of one sage who believed that all a fallen rider had to do was bend over, face the charging Longhorns, hold his hat firmly in his teeth, and shake his coat-tails over his back. One falling horse flung its rider on top of the racing animals who carried him some distance on the platform they provided. He had only a few bruises to show for his ride after he had rolled off to safety.

Some stampedes were deliberately started by rustlers and Indians, as if there were not enough natural causes to go around, while others were caused by practical jokes. And James Cook, author of *Fifty Years on the Old Frontier*, once decided to try and get close enough to a wild-eyed cow to touch it. He triumphed, but the result was a stampede of the whole herd. Some said that a herd could be set off by a hand blowing his nose.

Just occasionally a herd was stampeded by the drover to avoid danger. Baylis John Fletcher's boss, George Arnett, once raced his cattle across a saline deposit on the Cimarron, which was so poisonous that a hundred cow carcases decorated the locality.

Men wounded in a stampede could hope for little doctoring unless there was an Army post or town nearby. As for the dead,

64: Putting the drop on a wild one. Here one cowboy keeps an eye on the 'rope corral' while his companion selects a particular if unwilling animal.
COURTESY THE ERWIN E. SMITH COLLECTION OF RANGE LIFE PHOTOGRAPHS, LIBRARY OF CONGRESS.

they had a simple burial without ceremony. The remains of a cowboy were laid in a grave on the lone prairie, wrapped in a blanket. Stones were put over the spot to keep away the coyotes – if there were any stones – and if he was lucky a simple wooden headpiece was raised over him. One song above all others commemorates the men who died in stampedes, *Little Joe the Wrangler*, the boy who met a man's death trying to get the leaders into a mill:

> The next morning just at daybreak, we found where his horse fell,
> Down in a washout twenty feet below;
> And beneath the horse, mashed to a pulp, his spur had rung the knell
> Was our little Texas stray, poor Wrangling Joe.

Joseph G. McCoy's vision had proved a winner, indeed, the Chisholm Trail was almost too crowded in 1870, with herds mixed up by stampedes and sheer weight of numbers at river crossings. But the cattlemen of Texas now had Kansas fever (emotional, not physical) and, to make things even better for them, there was a rate war on the Chicago-New York lines. Before it finished, some companies were carrying Longhorns free of charge, this at a time when Texans were making between fifteen and twenty-five dollars on every Longhorn: each was worth forty dollars in Chicago and more in New York and the other big Eastern cities. 300,000 went up the trail in 1870, half going East by railroad, the rest either being held back to fatten for later sale or being driven to Wyoming, Montana and Dakota, where a vast new cattle country was opening up. And meanwhile other Kansas towns were beginning to get some of the action, centres like Wichita, Ellsworth, Newton, and, later, Dodge City and Caldwell.

Herds driven to the Canadian line would be on the trail from March until August if they had started in southern Texas, but the average time taken from the Red River crossing to the Kansas cowtowns was around thirty-five days. When the drover and his men reached the vicinity of a cowtown he first selected a good grazing place not too far from the town. There were citizens ready to place herds – such was the forethought of McCoy and his colleagues – where they would cause least aggravation to the small number of settlers in the Abilene area, and when the site was found a permanent camp was made. Then it was time to hope for buyers, preferably when the cattle had had a chance to fatten on the succulent Kansan grass. The first Texans who went up the trail liked being paid in gold, not Yankee greenbacks, despite the fact that they were not worthless like Confederate ones. Suspicions died hard and Northern buyers went out of their way to accommodate them. What the

65: A pose that particularly inspired artists and depicts a cowboy at full gallop, and its rider about to 'build a loop' on his lariat.
COURTESY ROBIN MAY COLLECTION.

hands did when they hit town is the subject of the next two chapters, not this one.

1871 was the greatest year of all on the Chisholm, for by the summer there were 600,000 cattle in south-central Kansas, which did Newton no harm, as Abilene was overwhelmed by the flood of Longhorns. In fact, the sheer amount of beef on the hoof was to lower the price, though, as we shall see in Chapter Five, the terrible winter of 1886-7 saw Nature redress the balance, help change the nature of the cattle trade, and virtually put an end to the great drives at a time when they were dying anyway for reasons to be discussed later.

But now, after months on the trail, and having survived numerous perils, the herd had arrived, its owner had negotiated its sale, and the cowboys had been paid. The frustrations of those weary months would soon be forgotten in a frenzy of excitement generated by strong drink, fast women and by games of chance. The cowboy was primed for action and the cowtown would make sure he had all he wanted – at a price.

66: The trail drive is over, the men paid off and their energies (and money) spent. Time once more to return home and await the next drive. These cowboys, photographed near Garden City Kansas in the late 1880s or 1890s were from New Mexico.
COURTESY KANSAS STATE HISTORICAL SOCIETY.

The cattle business, as seen by the Wichita *Weekly Beacon* in June and July, 1873:

June 4

Mrs. T. M. Boreland of Texas, with three children, is stopping at the Planter house. She is the happy possessor of about one hundred head of cattle, and accompanied the herd all the way from its starting point to this place, giving evidence of a pluck and business tact far superior to many of the 'lords'.

Jim Reed sold his herd right out last Saturday, having made a clearance inside of a week from the date of his arrival with the cattle. Buyers are coming in already from the eastern states, and the market promises infinitely better this than last year.

The following herds and herders have arrived since last Friday: O. S. Dean and Ray Dean, on Friday last, with the herds of C. S. Morrow and Sam Johnson, from Georgetown, Williamson County, Texas; L. B. Harris, up with Geo. Crain's herd from San Antonio, 1,000 beeves; J. E. Taylor, 1,500 beeves, from Jackson county, Texas; James Bryden, 1,020 head of beeves from Corpus Christi; S. S. Burchfield, Uvalde county, Texas, 900; H. C. Griner & Bro. of Uvalde county, 800 heads.

July 9

We regret to announce the painful news that Mrs. Boreland, the widow lady who came up with her three little children, died at the Planters [sic] house Saturday evening, with mania, superinduced by her long, tedious journey and over taxation of the brain. She had become endeared to many acquaintances here on account of her lady like character. Her remains were sent to Victoria, Texas, her former home on Tuesday evening last. Her affairs are in the hands of her own kin as also her children. Everything was done by relatives and friends to smooth the rapid current of the dark rolling river.

3

THE MURDEROUS TEXANS

A correspondent for the Toledo, Ohio, *Blade* visited Ellsworth in 1872, and one of the sights prompted this tongue-in-cheek comment:

> I noticed one young fellow fixed out in so many colors, I fancied he must belong to a circus, but was informed he was a TEXAS DROVER. He was certainly gorgeous, and I have no doubt he enjoyed to the fullest extent the attention we gave him – his hat was fancifully braided straw, and around the crown was a string of gaudy beads; each bead was as large as a marble. His jacket was made to hang open in front, so that his shirt, made of as many colors as Joseph's coat of old, might be allowed to add to the general effect. His trowsers [*sic*] had silver lace down the seams, and were tucked in his boots so that they would not hide the boots, which were striped with red morocco, running up and down the legs.

But for those who lived in the early cowtowns reality was quite different. Abilene as the first major cowtown was naturally

67: This woodcut appeared in *Frank Leslie's Illustrated Weekly* on 27 July 1878 and was entitled 'Texas Cattle in Dodge City'. However, it is sheer fiction, for it was rare for Longhorns to invade the actual cattle town streets. Had they done so, the result could have led to stampedes – of both citizens and cattle!
COURTESY THE KANSAS STATE HISTORICAL SOCIETY.

where the legend of the Texas cowboy first received general attention. The typical cowboy who appeared at Abilene between 1867 and 1872, was later described as a 'cow puncher,' 'cow prodder,' and 'steer-sticker,' by old-timers who had witnessed his exploits. But without exception they were generally called 'murderous Texans' and with good reason. Most of them were young, inexperienced, particularly in the ways of women, liquor and gambling, and they were easy pickings for the pimps, sharks and prostitutes who preyed upon them. Consequently, this psychological disadvantage aggravated their baser instincts and their reaction was violent.

On arrival, after several months on the trail, the herder's clothing was verminous and frequently in rags. He appeared undernourished, for his exposure to the elements, constant lack of sleep, and poor food had played havoc with his health. But once in town he revived his jaded spirits with a bath, a haircut and a complete change of clothing.

The thick woollen shirt, coarse trousers and working clothes of the trail gave way to fancy suits, stout corduroy fringed buckskin 'pants' and a huge sombrero 'it would take a day to walk round the brim of'. Around his neck, loosely tied, was a large bandanna kerchief of whatever colour suited him. His small waist was girthed by a gunbelt from which hung one or usually two revolvers in holsters that flapped when he walked.

In place of the heavy working boots, he forced his feet into knee high boots of the finest kid. Fitted with extra high heels, and sometimes embellished with the Lone Star set in the tops, they were designed for effect rather than comfort. Since walking was an exercise no self-respecting Texan indulged in in public, this combined with the high heels produced a shambling motion

68: Cowboys arriving in town and announcing their arrival with a few pistol shots, from a drawing by Remington.
COURTESY ROBIN MAY COLLECTION.

as he meandered, toed-in, shoulders slumped forward, along the uneven sidewalks or across rut-strewn streets. This wobbling motion made him look like an old man, and seemed oddly out of place with the display of colour, armament and the huge rowels on his spurs which jingled loudly as he walked.

The cowboy's attachment to his 'shootin' irons' was a feature that caused most concern. The Topeka *Daily Commonwealth* on 15 August 1871 noted that the Texan would use his revolvers 'with as little hesitation on a man as on a wild animal. Such a character is dangerous and desperate, and each one generally has killed his man. There are good and even honorable men among them, but run-away boys and men who find it too hot for them even in Texas join the cattle drovers and constitute a large proportion of them. They drink, swear, and fight; and life with them is a round of boisterous gaiety and indulgence in sensual pleasure.'

Never a character to appear modest, the cowboy took great delight in pandering to his reputation. In Abilene, before law and order was established, his arrival was heralded by a fusilade of pistol shots. Writing in 1910, Theophilus Little, an early resident recalled:

> All the cattle were herded west of town. Every cowboy that came into town had to pass my office door. There were hundreds of them every day and every 'son of a gun' had *two* guns and I thought every gun was as long as an Ohio fence rail. These boys came into town and did not leave Texas street, [they] would drink and gamble, get rip-roaring crazy drunk and towards evening jump [upon] their Texas ponies and then begin to shoot hundreds of shots, yelling like a million Indians, ponies on the dead run. Every boy passed my office and by the time they got there the air was lurid as they shot upwards. At first I would run to the door to see the show, but I soon learned to crawl into a hole and pull the hole in after me or pull a pile of lumber over on to me. Then down into the creek and up the west bank and disappear over on the unlimited prairie and then back next day and repeat.

Not surprisingly early residents feared the cowboy. Stuart Henry, who grew up in Abilene, having arrived there as a seven-year-old in 1868, recalled the 'cowboy' as a creature who had little or no respect for law and order, religion or God, and who in manner was profane, gross, vulgar and obscene. Few decent women had crossed his path, and he seemed to exist on a diet of 'chawed' or smoked tobacco and 'poison' whisky. His knife and gun were his constant companions and he was prone to use these 'toys' at the least provocation. As the mood took him, he unlimbered his 'artillery' and fired at anything that moved.

Understandably, townspeople believed that the cowboy was as unpredictable as a Longhorn bull, and that he had no compunction about killing when 'liquored up'. Some recalled that a

69: Cowboys had a fine, if macabre, sense of humour. In this contemporary sketch the worried bartender is being told he liked his liquor – fill 'im up!
COURTESY ROBIN MAY COLLECTION.

man who incurred the enmity of a drunken trail-driving companion took care to avoid exposing himself to a bullet in the back, fired through the door or a window of a saloon or from the darkness.

Few of the actual drovers or stockmen engaged in such antics, and most of them avoided the places where such violence was an accepted part of a day or night's entertainment. Yet they sometimes fell foul of their own cowboys. Writing in 1874, Joseph G. McCoy recalled an incident in 1868 when a party of drovers were taking a late night walk before retiring to the Drovers' Cottage. Suddenly, a 'mounted, crazy, drunk cow-boy was upon them', yelling in a maniacal voice for them to halt, and racing around them firing his revolvers over their heads. He demanded money, but they managed to evade him, and one rushed to his room to get his pistols and deal with him, but by then the cowboy had galloped off into the dark, robbed a gambling house and disappeared out across the prairie.

The rot-gut whisky loosely described as 'bitters' in contemporary advertisements as being among 'choice' liquors, was only one of the temptations extended to the cowboy. Dancing was an accomplishment few possessed, but once 'lubricated' the cowboy willingly engaged in it with a zest that was quite remarkable. His huge spurs jangled at every step and frequently wrought havoc with the dress hems of his luckless partners. And with his hat tilted back and his odd shuffling and jumping motion, he cut a comic figure. His revolvers flapped up and down like 'a retreating sheep's tail', recalled McCoy, and with his 'eyes lit up with excitement, liquor and lust; he plunges in and "hoes it down" at a terrible rate, in the most approved yet awkward country style; often swinging "his partner" clear off the floor for an entire circle, then "balance all" with an occa-

70: **Cowtown entertainment catered for all tastes, and a popular pastime was dancing – spurs, gun and all!**
COURTESY THE KANSAS STATE HISTORICAL SOCIETY.

sional demonic yell, near akin to the war whoop of the savage Indian. All this he does, entirely oblivious to the whole world "and the balance of mankind". After dancing furiously, the entire "set" is called to "waltz to the bar", where the boy is required to treat his partner. . . .'

The 'partner' was usually a prostitute or 'hostess' whose sole ambition was to have a good time with as little expense to herself as possible. The women who flocked to the cowtowns are today a legend themselves. They came from all walks of life, were of many races and vied with their male counterparts – the gamblers, pimps, cardsharps and some saloon-keepers—to make as much money as possible in the short time available during the season.

These 'ladies' frequently outshone the cowboy in sartorial splendour. Few were avid readers of *Godey's Lady's Book* or the illustrated weeklies; but somehow they maintained the height of fashion curiously out of place in the dust, heat and drabness that personified the cowtowns. Voluminous skirts hung on built-in frames, 'cages' or 'bustles' which when she walked offered tantalising sights of multi-coloured petticoats worn beneath. Like the cowboy, she wore high boots of the finest kid, and the high-heeled narrow-toed fit produced the same effect: when she walked she hobbled, and her tight bodice and large bustle made her appear deformed.

71: 'Timberline' was a typical Dodge City prostitute.
COURTESY THE KANSAS STATE HISTORICAL SOCIETY.

But those boots served a dual purpose: among the gaudy clusters of tassles flowing from the deeply scalloped tops, surmounted by a gleaming Lone Star, she carried two items essential to her well-being. In one reposed her purse and in the other a pistol (sometimes ornately engraved or jewelled) or a knife. Armed in this manner she was not only potentially dangerous, but her weapons protected her life, her independence

72.

and prevented her from fraud. Curiously, she placed her self-respect above anything else, yet allowed sometimes perverted liberties with her body.

The cowtown 'doves' or 'sisters-in-sin' were a hard lot. Faces which were once pretty soon became hard and lined, and they only maintained colour by liberal use of rouge and powder. But it was their eyes which more than anything reflected the depravity of their existence. Hard, haunted and ever watchful, they rarely looked one in the face for long, and when such a woman smiled, her eyes remained cold and dead.

Some of the women had also 'killed their man', and if anything were as hard or harder than their male companions. This is no exaggeration. In December 1869, at Junction City, a huge 'six-foot American citizen of African descent, hideous to behold', and variously known as 'Black Sal', 'Swamp Angel', and 'Straight Edge', according to the Topeka *Weekly Commonwealth*, was disturbed in bed early one Sunday morning by drunken troops from nearby Fort Riley. When they refused to leave, 'Sal' pulled a pistol and shot four of them, two of whom died. The local wits immediately dubbed her 'Wild Bill No. 2', for 'better shooting was never done under the circumstances'.

But such extremes were rare. Most cowtown women were more subtle. However, few hesitated to rob would-be customers, and a man 'addled by drink', and driven by a lust confused by an alcoholic haze, without his gun or trousers, stood little chance against a devious cold sober 'dove'! Even when brawls broke out in saloons, dance-halls or brothels, it was not unknown for women to join in. Yet these same women knew well enough that they were at a premium and were outnumbered by their 'customers' ten to one—sometimes in even greater numbers.

The women who populated Abilene's Texas Street, Newton's 'Hide Park' and similar red-light districts, were a very mixed breed. Most of them were young, and after a comparatively short period left the game altogether (some even married former customers); but there were a very limited number who stayed on until their forties, by which time they displayed the ravages of time, disease and desperation. How they embarked on such a hazardous existence was often a tragedy in itself. For some the lure of the bright lights of the West had been the only escape from the humdrum existence of the settled East, and too late they realised that they had made a terrible mistake.

72: 'Squarrel-tooth Alice' of Dodge City was one of the better looking ladies of uneasy virtue. It is uncertain if the squirrel on her lap is a prop or a pet.
COURTESY THE KANSAS STATE HISTORICAL SOCIETY.

Advertisements for 'waitresses' and other domestics with one way tickets had imprisoned many. Destitute and without any friends or the means to escape, they were compelled to adapt to a life that conflicted with moral and social upbringings. Some could not take the life and resorted to suicide. The more worldly of their customers, while appreciating their physical attributes as a means of satisfying a need, treated them with contempt. And when a saloon girl made the mistake of actually liking or falling in love with a customer, her feelings were rarely reciprocated. For some, time was a great healer, but for others there was the desperation of a 'woman scorned' and retribution, or suicide. For those that survived the perils and passions of prostitution, luck sometimes played a part; but the hard-core brigade often became 'madams' in high-class whorehouses. In such positions they were able to control the lives and destinies of the less fortunate, at the same time protecting themselves against unwanted custom or intrusion.

Allied with the women of the cowtowns in their efforts to fleece the Texans and others unwise enough to put themselves in their clutches, were the gamblers, pimps, and saloon-keepers. They descended like locusts upon the cowtowns. Their saloons and dance-halls mushroomed wherever the trade went. Mostly one-roomed establishments with large, painted false-fronts embellished with gaudy signs and lit up at night by harsh kerosene lamps, the early cowtown saloon looked like an oasis in an otherwise arid desert. The proprietors furthered this illusion: well dressed in expensive 'boiled' white shirts with diamond studs, silk waistcoats and cravats, they toured their domain with a permanent, humourless smile, and kept a wary eye upon the activities of staff and customer alike. Behind the bar was an arsenal of weapons within easy access in case of trouble, and few men, drunk or sober, cared to back down an irate saloon-keeper armed with a sawn-off shotgun.

Concerned at the rise in crimes associated with gambling, the editor of the Abilene *Chronicle* on 1 June 1871 published an Exchange item headed 'Gambling' which graphically described the tricks employed by professional gamblers to 'come it' over 'suckers' whom they fleeced with monotonous regularity. The two-column article detailed the tricks employed in such games as Roulette, Rouge et Noir, Vingt et Un, and Poker. Every imaginable trick from marked cards, fixed wheels, and mirrors on the knees to 'reflect' upon another man's hand whilst it was being dealt during single games of poker. Again, superstitious gamblers who insisted upon having a wall at their backs were often the victims of deceit. Sometimes the 'wall' was a cover for a box or room in which a man or a boy spied on them and by means of wires fixed to a plank or board under the foot of the house 'sharp' could 'telegraph' the victim's 'hand'! Nonetheless, gambling continued to reap huge profits in the cowtowns, and was responsible for many gunfights.

73: Frederic Remington's 'Making a Tenderfoot Dance' was amusing to all but a tenderfoot. Fortunately, such incidents (and injuries) were rare!
COURTESY ROBIN MAY COLLECTION.

Wedged in between this nightmare of depravity were the honest God-fearing 'civilians' anxious only to go about their business without incurring the enmity of either side. Merchants who opened stores were well aware of the dangers. Before law and order were established in Abilene, it was not uncommon for a storekeeper to fall foul of a drunken Texan, and to be beaten up, his store wrecked, and perhaps himself shot. Pitched battles on the street between drunken cowboys, were the signal for everyone else to make themselves scarce or hug the floor and pray.

The cattle season lasted roughly from May to October, but

once the drovers, stockmen and cowboys had departed until the following season, a hush descended upon the cowtowns. Ellsworth, which had been established several years before its entry into the trade, did not notice the change in quite the same way that Abilene or Newton did. Newton got into the cattle business during the summer of 1871 when the Santa Fe Railway reached the place, and by late August its saloons, gambling and dance-halls outnumbered Abilene's. But once the season ended, the same exodus of 'sinful humanity' was seen en route to St Louis and Kansas City and other places to await the new season.

74: The drovers and buyers dealt strictly in cash, and here we see the interior of the Caldwell Stock Exchange bank 1881. Dare we say it, but is that a *lady* staring through the grill marked *CHANGE?*
COURTESY THE KANSAS STATE HISTORICAL SOCIETY.

During the cattle season, and despite the obvious perils and the dramatic rise in population, life in a cowtown was never dull. But once winter came, and the population dropped to hundreds, the citizens were faced with utter boredom and their cities resembled ghost towns. Abilene's Texas Street was practically deserted. Paint peeled from the walls of saloon and brothel as the roughhewn unseasoned planks of hastily constructed buildings were exposed to the elements. Sidewalks, too, showed similar haste. Uneven and made from still-green wood, they soon warped and bent with changes in the weather, and unwary walkers tripped and cursed over projecting nails or loose boards. Sudden gaps between buildings, or unsuspected steps meant a constant change in height and sometimes a bad fall for the careless. During the winter the dust of summer gave way to mud which soon became a mire when churned up by horse and wagon, and the only access from one side of the street to the other for the less hardy was by planks strewn across the mud.

Since entertainment during the season had been confined

75: St. Louis, Mo. was involved in the cattle business before the Civil War. This interesting view was published in the *Illustrated London News* on 1 May 1858.
COURTESY 'ILLUSTRATED LONDON NEWS'.

76: Wichita, Kansas, in 1878, at a time when the cattle business (for her) was on the wane and civilisation on the increase.
COURTESY THE KANSAS STATE HISTORICAL SOCIETY.

mostly to the Texan part of town (including in Abilene's case the Novelty Theatre), little attention was paid to similar pursuits for the permanent citizens. The resultant boredom was relieved in many ways, sometimes violent, but mostly simple things that catered for the human need for communication. It became common for people to gather at the depot morning and evening, and occasionally at noon, to witness the arrival of both passenger and freight trains. The appearance of out-of-town newspapers was always an event, and the few passengers that disembarked were always welcome.

Then came the spring, and with it the return of the Texans and others. First came the merchants to re-open their stores, restock them with clothing and other goods, and in their wake the saloon-keepers and the others ready to prey upon the incoming herders. The cowtown was back in business.

4

TAMING THE TEXANS

'WHEN you heard one or two shots, you waited breathlessly for a third. A third shot meant a death on Texas Street,' recalled Stuart Henry, whose boyhood was spent during cowtown Abilene's rise from nothing to become the 'wickedest city in America'.

Memories of drink-crazed Texans galloping up and down the streets, swaying in their saddles, cursing and firing pistols, remained with him for his whole life. Yet miraculously few of the citizens who stepped gingerly about their daily business were actually attacked. But the ever-present danger was there, and even some of the Texans reacted against their own kind. One recalled being on hand when a drunken cowboy rode his horse into a saloon, pulled his pistol and forced the crowd to leave in a panic. Whisky flowed like water, and was of a quality that would 'make rabbits fight a bulldog'.

Coupled with the ever growing gambling and prostitution, was the very real fear of disaster unless it was checked. Late in 1869 a number of Abilene's more responsible citizens organised a committee, and they petitioned the probate judge of Dickinson County for incorporation. He agreed and the place was rated a 'third-class' city with the power to hold elections. A number of trustees were appointed until a proper election could be held, and by May 1870, they had created the position of Marshal.

77: Theodore C. Henry, first mayor of Abilene, and the man who hired Tom Smith as its first marshal in 1870.
COURTESY THE KANSAS STATE HISTORICAL SOCIETY.

Theodore C. Henry, elder brother of Stuart, was appointed acting Mayor, and it was his choice of Marshal that proved to be the salvation of Abilene, and at the same time gave birth to a myth—the lone man against the mob.

The man chosen by Henry to keep the peace in Abilene was Thomas James Smith, who he later stated was the celebrated 'Bear River' Tom Smith whom had played a big part in the riots at Bear Town (or River), Wyoming in 1868 when he was a trouble-shooter for the Union Pacific Railway. According to the *Deseret News* that Tom Smith had been arrested and sent to the state penitentiary; but if Henry was right, and it was the same man, he was now free and in Abilene. The 1870 Census gives Smith's age as forty and 'born in New York' which meant the state rather than the city, but little else is known of his origin.

Contemporary newspaper reports and the memories of old-timers show that Tom Smith, who used his sledgehammer fists rather than his pistols, achieved a respect for law and order many thought impossible. His reliance upon his fists instead of his two silver-mounted Colt revolvers baffled and demoralised the gun-toting Texans who, as noted earlier, tended to despise fist-fighters. They could not afford to despise Tom Smith.

Tom Smith so affected Henry that in later years when describing how he had sworn in the new Marshal, he intimated that the sun blazing across Smith's shoulder and into his eyes was almost halo-like. Nonetheless, Smith did what he was paid for and kept the Texans in check until the season ended. Tragically, he was murdered by two settlers when attempting to arrest one of them for murder at the request of the local sheriff who was too ill to do it himself.

Following several months of doubt and the employment of stop-gap policemen, in April 1871 the city held its first municipal election. Joseph G. McCoy was elected as Mayor and one of his first tasks was to organise a police force capable of tackling the incoming Texans. His choice of James Butler 'Wild Bill' Hickok as Marshal was 'unanimously' accepted by the council, and on 15 April Wild Bill took office.

78: Thomas James Smith, Marshal of Abilene in 1870: the first man to teach the Texans respect for law and order. From a tintype discovered in the 1890s and copied by the Abilene photographer, Forney.
COURTESY THE KANSAS STATE HISTORICAL SOCIETY.

79: James Butler 'Wild Bill' Hickok, from a photograph by Charles Smith, Topeka, circa 1868. When Marshal of Abilene in 1871, he was one of the 'sights' for visiting Texans, and most of them went in awe of him, for his reputation with a pistol was well known on the trail.
COURTESY THE KANSAS CITY STATE HISTORICAL SOCIETY.

Wild Bill Hickok was the complete antithesis of Tom Smith. Where Smith had relied upon his fists and forceful personality, Hickok left no one in any doubt that if he had to he would draw his pistols. Some claimed that this was because his 'bravery was of a far lower type' and that 'without his pistols he would have been tame', but the truth was that Hickok was well able to use his fists – and proved it on occasions. The difference between the two men was basic: Hickok won his reputation with a gun, and to survive he had to continue to use one. Yet despite his reputation as the premier 'two-gun' man of the frontier, Wild Bill rarely resorted to those pistols, relying for the most part upon his already snowballing legend to subdue would-be troublemakers and glory hunters. In fact, it was only toward the end of his reign as Abilene's Marshal that he actually used his pistols to restore order.

Thus, the image of the town Marshal and his function is a composite of both the Hickok and Smith tradition. In truth, the reality is something of each, and this coupled with the reputations of the places and the men they were expected to 'tame' has greatly influenced not only present-day reaction, but is reflected in the attitudes of the old-timers themselves.

Abilene grew from almost nothing to become the leading cattle-trading centre of the plains, and its reputation for violence grew with it. But other cowtowns suffered from their reputations long before they entered into the trade. Ellsworth was the most notorious. It was founded in 1867 and for three years was overflowing with a motley collection of teamsters, soldiers, buffalo hunters, army scouts, railroad workers, and the inevitable prostitutes and gamblers. Its close proximity to Fort Harker was partly responsible for such a varied humanity, and perhaps another reason why the violence, although very

79.

evident, never grew bad enough to prompt the local Post Commander to threaten martial law, as had the Commander of Fort Hays following riots in May 1869. By the time the cattle trade reached the place in large numbers in 1871, the city was already governed by a council backed by a strong police force, and under the watchful eye of the county sheriff.

Newton on the other hand, was Abilene all over again. As we have mentioned, by August 1871 it boasted twenty-seven saloons and a population of 1,500 which included a large number of prostitutes. One newspaper correspondent doubted that there were a dozen 'virtuous women' in the whole place. Attempts to impose law and order were met with resistance, and despite much violence this was eventually achieved.

Dodge City was established in 1872, four years before the cattle trade arrived, and like its neighbours had suffered the antics of innumerable transients, the majority of them buffalo

80: Dodge City's citizens turned out en masse for this photograph circa 1873. As yet the cattle business had still to boom, and most of the town's prosperity relied upon the buffalo hunters.
COURTESY KANSAS STATE HISTORICAL SOCIETY.

hunters who made the town their headquarters. Dodge had been in existence only months when it was in the grip of a band of local terrorists masquerading as 'vigilantes'. Their antics grew so serious that in December 1872 the local commandant from Fort Dodge was forced to send in troops.

In Wichita, where the Chisholm Trail officially ended, and which, but for the lack of a railroad, might well have been the first major Kansas cowtown, law and order had also been slow starters. However, when the railroad arrived and with it the cattle trade, the local editor expressed the concern felt by all that there should be law and order, and with it peace and security and 'not bloodshed and a name that will cause a thrill of horror whenever mentioned and which will effectually deter the most desirable class of people from coming among us. Right speedily will the latter follow if the former are not maintained.' A brave reaction at a time when according to one report 'anything goes in Wichita'.

Much later, Caldwell, which entered the cattle trade right at the end of the era, achieved a degree of violence that in some measure surpassed the worst days of early Abilene and Dodge. But perhaps because it appeared late on the scene, the place never quite achieved the reputation of its better publicised rivals.

As each town took on the cattle business it was faced with the same problem of controlling violence. Despite volumes of fiction, hundreds of films and 'recollections' to the contrary, no Texan or any other individual convicted of murder in the cowtowns was hanged legally in Kansas during the period covered by our study. Many men were jailed for various crimes, but those who died were either lynched, shot or knifed during personal or community quarrels. And as far as local punishments were concerned, town councils became adept at imposing

81: Wichita in 1873 at the height of her period as a cowtown.
COURTESY THE KANSAS STATE HISTORICAL SOCIETY.

fines for 'misdemeanours' which sufficed to placate local reaction, yet at the same time did not antagonise the promoters of the cattle trade. Many reasoned that if the city fathers grew too harsh the trade would be taken elsewhere. While some, notably the farmers, welcomed such a move, storekeepers, with few exceptions, sought to keep the trade, for their business and profits soared when the herds reached town. Nonetheless, both factions realised only too well that there had to be controls, and various methods were tried to enforce them.

When the Abilene council created the post of marshal in May 1870, they also implemented a number of ordinances aimed at curtailing gambling, prostitution, vagrancy, and the 'keeping of houses of ill-fame'. Firearms were banned and fines imposed for carrying or discharging them within city limits—or a term in jail. The editor of the *Chronicle* noted that 'heretofore the Texans have not been interferred with much, by the officers of the law in this locality [Dickinson County] when they killed each other', and demanded that henceforth they be treated like everyone else under the law. The editor also condemned the men who carried and used pistols as 'uncivilised'. But as Hickok and Smith learned when they tried to enforce anti-firearm laws, it was impossible totally to disarm everyone. Even a Kansas law forbidding the carrying of arms by former Confederates and other 'Rebels' was completely unenforceable. Only the threat of retaliation or a reputation kept most trouble-makers in check.

A facet of the upsurge of law and order in the cowtowns was the power mayors had to impose the Kansas Code upon all male inhabitants between the ages of eighteen and fifty to help him enforce the law. This was very rarely used and only then when regular law enforcement had broken down or was unenforceable. Two incidents in particular stand out that prompted the ringing of the fire bell or the police bell summoning the populace armed with all manner of weapons. The first was in 1874 when on 6 July William A. 'Hurricane Bill' Martin and some cronies 'treed' Wichita. A policeman named Samuel Botts tried to arrest a drunken Texan when Hurricane Bill and his gang were racing up and down the streets taking pot shots at anybody and anything. Someone rang the police bell and fifty armed citizens appeared on the street. City Marshal William Smith then tried to persuade both sides to back off peacefully, but the

82. Four Oregon Cowboys.
COURTESY OREGON HISTORICAL SOCIETY.

situation was only resolved when S. M. Tucker, a lawyer, offered to arrest someone. Smith pointed at Martin and said: 'Arrest Hurricane Bill!' Tucker promptly cocked his shotgun and thrust the barrels into Martin's stomach. Hurricane Bill admitted he was beaten and dropped his pistols, as did his companions.

A similar situation occurred in Ellsworth in August 1873 when Ben Thompson and his homicidal brother Bill had a row with fellow Texans and the local police. Ben's friend Chauncey B. Whitney, the county sheriff, tried to intercede and he was shot down by a drunken Billy without any provocation. He used Ben's handsome handmade English shotgun by George Gibbs of Bristol, and Whitney's terrible scream sobered all who heard it. Billy later claimed it was an accident, but while Ben held the town at bay he escaped on horseback and made his way to Texas. Meantime, Whitney was carried to his home where he

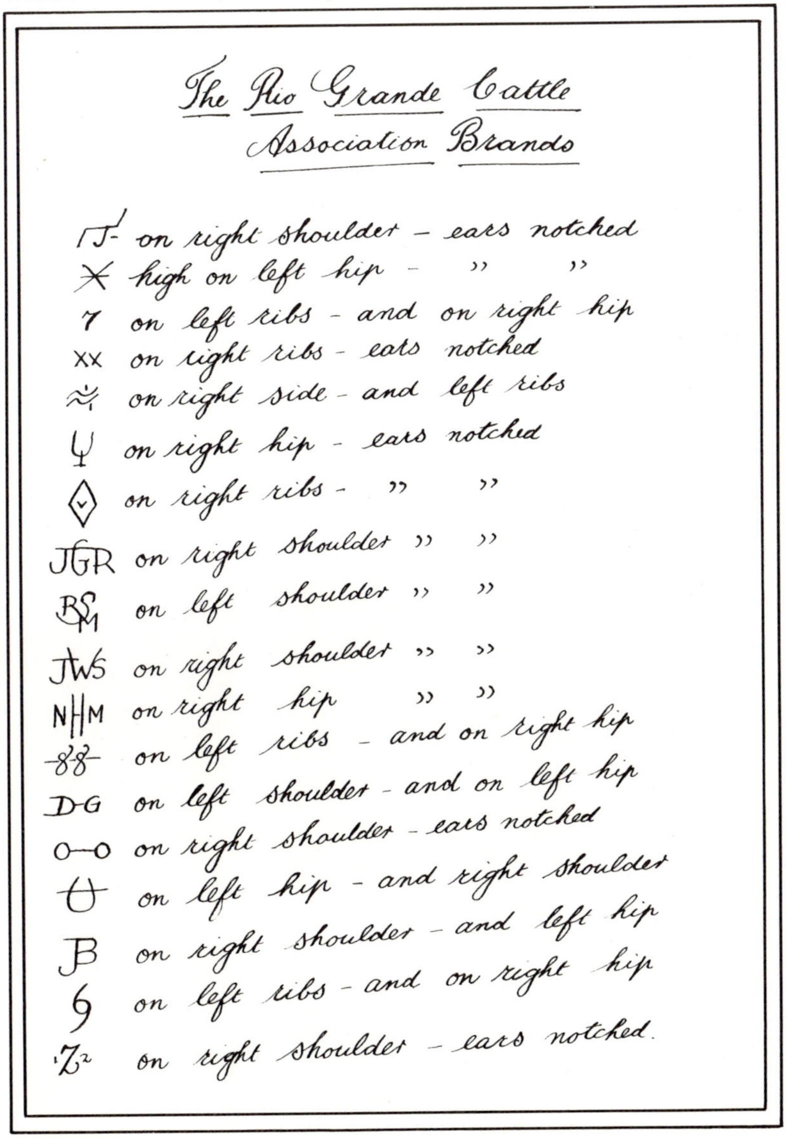
The Rio Grande Cattle Association Brands

on right shoulder – ears notched
high on left hip – " "
7 on left ribs – and on right hip
XX on right ribs – ears notched
on right side – and left ribs
on right hip – ears notched
on right ribs – " "
JGR on right shoulder " "
on left shoulder " "
JWS on right shoulder " "
NHM on right hip " "
-88- on left ribs – and on right hip
DG on left shoulder – and on left hip
O–O on right shoulder – ears notched
on left hip – and right shoulder
JB on right shoulder – and left hip
6 on left ribs – and on right hip
on right shoulder – ears notched.

83: Cattle brands were like signatures and this list although fictitious, does nonetheless depict the various means employed to establish ownership.
COURTESY JOSEPH G. ROSA WESTERN AMERICANA COLLECTION

lingered for three days before dying in great agony. The Mayor was so disgusted that he fired the town's police force with the exception of Edward O. Hogue who had made the arrest when Ben finally agreed to give up his gun if the others were disarmed also. Brother Billy was later brought back for trial, but was acquitted much to the disgust of the citizens who believed that the jury had been bought.

Ironically, only the day before the fatal shooting of Whitney, the Editor of the *Reporter* had remarked as part of a growing, but premature 'civilised' attitude toward police methods that:

> We protest against so much arming by our police. It may be well enough for our marshal and his assistants to go armed,

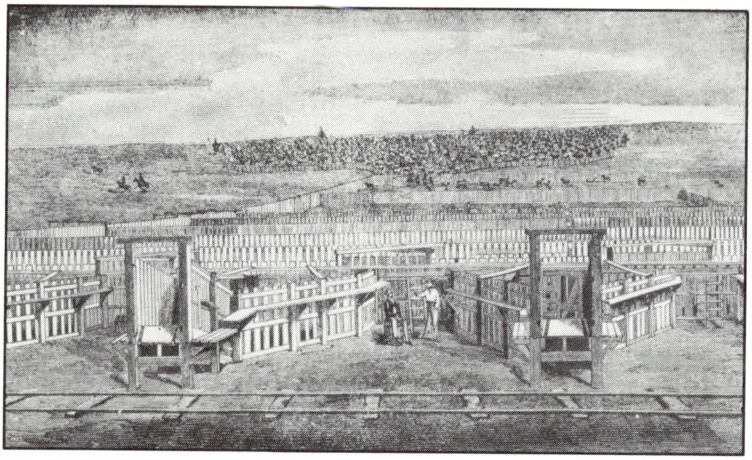

84. The Ellsworth shipping pens, circa 1873, from a woodcut made for McCoy's *Historic Sketches*. The cattle can be seen arriving.
COURTESY ROBIN MAY COLLECTION.

85: Leading cattle into pens was one thing, controlling them another.
COURTESY ROBIN MAY COLLECTION.

but one six shooter is enough. It is too much to have to see double armed men walking our peaceful streets. It is not probable that any of the shotted revolvers will hurt anyone, for these are not the days of '67 and all people know. Don't let us by too big a show of deringers [*sic*], lead strangers to imagine that order is only to be maintained by the use of them. One pistol is enough and that should be concealed as much as possible.

But such individual disruption of a whole town was very rare. For the most part the cattle-trading centres were able to rely upon their police forces to keep order. The Marshal or Chief of Police normally had one or two regular deputies, but during the cattle season several others were employed to keep the peace in the brothel districts or add strength on patrol duties. The checking of guns was also tackled in various ways. Some were handed into the marshal's office, or pushed across the bar of a saloon, while in Wichita, in 1871, the marshal was ordered to erect two signboards warning visitors that weapons were strictly forbidden. A year later the toll collectors employed on the privately owned Chisholm Trail bridge were sworn in as special deputies. They were then empowered to disarm all incoming visitors and give them a metal token in exchange. By 1873 this scheme was abandoned and the signboards were back advising their visitors to leave their revolvers 'at police headquarters, and get a check'.

Dodge City experienced similar reactions against the carrying of firearms and, in 1873, let it be known that any persons found carrying 'concealed weapons in the city of Dodge or

86: 'Prodders' at work in a Kansas City packing house, driving cattle in from the pens to be slaughtered.
COURTESY ROBIN MAY COLLECTION.

violating the laws of the State shall be dealt with according to law'.

Easily enough said, but difficult to implement, especially when it is remembered that the transient population always outnumbered the local police and civilians. For every man that was prepared to surrender his gun, there was someone who preferred to conceal it. Not always to cause trouble, but because he seriously believed he might need it and without it he was virtually defenceless.

Incidents that took place in cowtowns concerned with firearms and their control are numerous, and some of them can be cited to emphasise the sometimes humorous, sometimes tragic and sometimes racial reaction they provoked.

On 4 June 1873, the Wichita *Weekly Beacon* noted that a

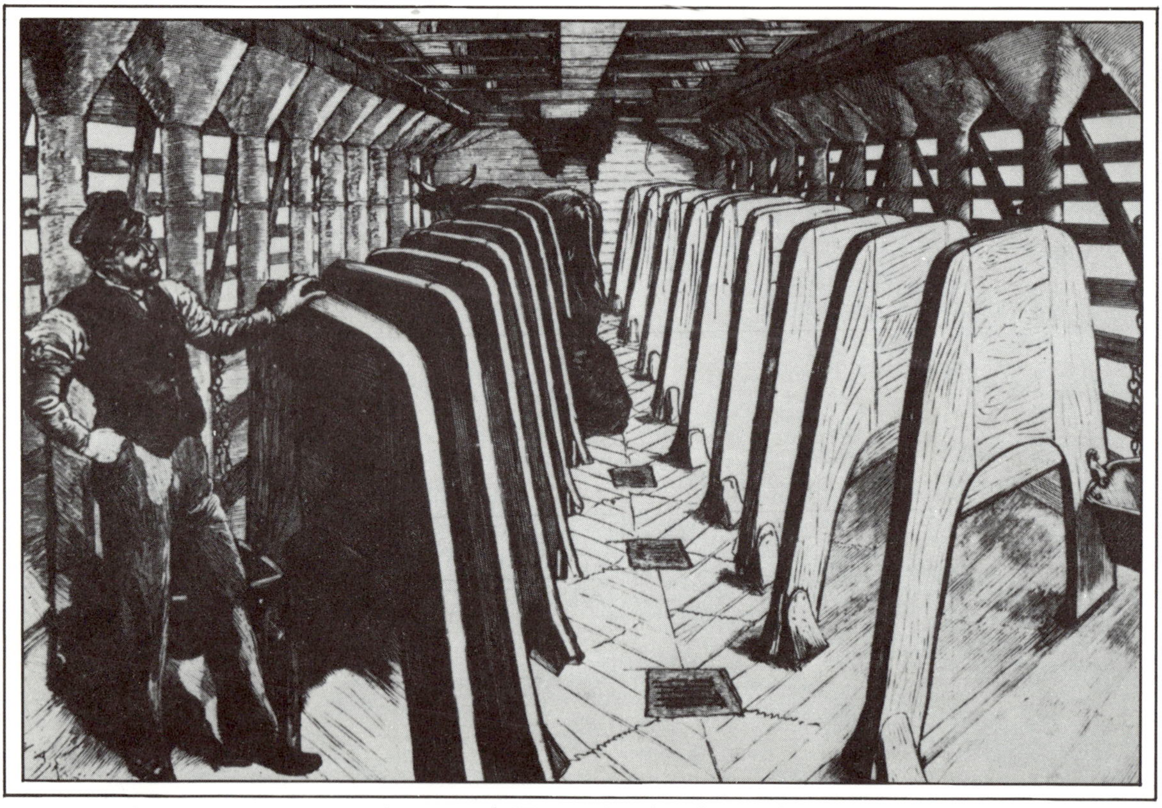

87: During the early years of the drives, cattle shipped East by rail had a pretty rough ride, and stops had to be made en route to feed and water them. But by 1881 individual stalls were being provided, and with proper feeding and drainage facilities, their lot was much more sanitary and humane.
COURTESY ROBIN MAY COLLECTION.

'mounted Texas herder in rapid transit passed the Avenue House Monday morning, jostled a six shooter out of the scabbard, it struck the ground, went off and sent a bullet through the steps of the hotel. Luckily no one happened to be sitting on the steps as is often the case.'

In August of the same year, it was reported that three 'herders' galloped along Douglas Avenue in Wichita flourishing pistols and defied the police to arrest them. Constable Cairns promptly stepped into the street and forced them to rein up. He arrested one of them who he thought was their leader, but a companion rode forward and said that he should arrest him first. Cairns reached for him and the man resisted, and Cairns immediately struck him 'over the head with a Navy'. Later, it was found that the fellow had suffered severe concussion and physicians believed he had also sustained brain damage from the effects of the 'iron that fell upon him'.

In reporting the incident the local press regretted the affair but felt there was no mild manner with which to restrain law-breakers:

> If however, there is any other way in the world to persuade infractors of the city laws to desist, aside from beating them over the head with a revolver, we insist that it should be resorted to, and the knock down business only used in self preservation. It is strange with the reputation our police have far and near, for reckless daring, grit and determination

> to duty, even at the sacrifice of life, and that anyone should attempt to infringe the law before them, after being told to desist, unless it is done to try their mettle.

88: A cattle train passing the famous Drover's Cottage at Ellsworth, from a woodcut made for McCoy's *Historic Sketches*.
COURTESY ROBIN MAY COLLECTION.

Only weeks before the *Beacon* had reported on 30 July a shooting affray that caused great excitement yet failed to provoke the police into action. Apparently, a Texas herder came into town, hitched his 'mule' in front of a store and before entering to make purchases, hung his revolver and belt upon the saddle horn. Minutes later, the mule 'put all his feet together and treated himself to a terrific shake, which brought the revolver in contact with the horn of the saddle, throwing back the hammer and sending a bullet through the holster into the ground'. During the panic which followed, the owner rushed out of the store and it was then realised what had happened. Gravely the editor noted that since there was no 'ordinance providing for the arrest of mules for discharging firearms', no arrest was made, and as for the mule he had fallen asleep!

Despite ordinances against the carrying of arms, there was little that could be done to stop disputes between Texans. In June 1872 the Wichita *Eagle* reported that a 'French Creole from Texas' had walked into a saloon with a cocked gun and approached a man named Anderson. But Anderson also held a cocked gun out of sight, and suddenly raised it and shot the Frenchman through the breast, and 'he was dead before he struck the floor. He was buried next morning on a sand island. Both men were intoxicated and were said to have been the best of friends.'

89: A typical advertisement of the trail-driving era to be found in the livestock journals.
COURTESY ROBIN MAY COLLECTION.

Racial conflicts were another problem. The number of Negroes who came up the trail as cowboys in the early days was far less than has been claimed recently; but the same could not be said for Mexicans. Many travelled with the herds or even brought up their own, and some settled in Kansas. Abilene experienced little trouble, but other places were not so fortunate. Latin temperaments, and a quick reaction to gun or knife – the latter weapon was a particular favourite and could be thrown with great speed and accuracy – did not always sit well with Texans who were open in their dislike of 'greasers'. For their part many of the *vaqueros* felt equally ill-at-ease with the 'Gringos' and, distrustful of paper money, requested all payments in silver.

Wichita seems to have been particularly unfortunate in its race relations. On 20 August 1873 the *Weekly Beacon* reported the murder of a Texan named Reddis who was shot by a Mexican following a dispute over gambling and a sum of money. Three of Reddis's 'herders' were said to be in pursuit of

90: Once the herd reached town it had to await its turn at the loading pens. Outside of Abilene and most other places, the drovers chose areas with suitable grazing and water.
COURTESY JOSEPH G. ROSA WESTERN AMERICANA COLLECTION.

the Mexican, and 'woe, will betide this diluted son of the Montezumas if they ever chance upon him'. But on the 27th the paper said that the murdered man was not Reddis but an employee named William Vickers, and that two Mexicans named Henria and Polora were responsible. The Texans caught them up at Skeleton Creek where Polora was killed by an irate stagecoach driver who had been shot through the hand by one of them and had promptly 'swung loose his arsenal and sped Polora's soul to its Maker. The other was killed on the spot in an attempt to resist an arrest, that at least is what they call it in these parts.'

In November the *Eagle* reported that 'a dozen Mexican greasers, camped upon the other side of the river', had attacked Constable Prentis and beat him with their revolvers 'almost inhumanly', and the sheriff was out with a posse to track them down and 'we have no doubt of their arrest and punishment'.

John Wesley Hardin in his *Life* recalled a fight he had had with Mexicans whilst en route to Abilene in 1871. Six of them were killed, and he and a companion later killed another one in revenge for the murder of a fellow Texan. Reading between the lines it is evident that little love was lost on both sides.

But more important to most early-day residents was the control of the gambling halls and saloons and brothels, some of which were in the middle of the residential district. In Abilene where most of these places were separated from 'decent' citizens by the tracks of the Kansas Pacific, there were still those who called for their removal. The Council were divided on the issue, well aware that an enormous revenue came from such places, and it was even alleged in the *Chronicle* that McCoy had suggested that all saloons should be charged $50 for a licence which was contrary to ordinances. Furious, '100 respectable ladies' threatened to rise up en masse and drive the women and gamblers out if ordinances were not enforced. A compromise was reached, and 'Texan Abilene' was moved to another part of town.

91: John Wesley Hardin was not a typical cowboy, but his antics on the way to and in Abilene served to publicise the more violent side of the 'terrible Texans'.
COURTESY JOSEPH G. ROSA WESTERN AMERICANA COLLECTION.

Anticipating opposition, the Council primed Marshal Hickok and his deputies to expect trouble, but the Texans seemed pleased with the arrangements, for it allowed them to continue their roistering without too much opposition.

But the move was only a prelude to the final solution later in the year when Hickok was ordered to close down all the brothels and gambling dens. The resultant emigration of 'vast numbers of sinful humanity – prostitutes, "pimps", "cappers", [gamblers' decoys] and others of a like ilk' may have delighted some citizens and local farmers, but it also meant the end of a lucrative trade, and led to Abilene's decline. The Texans later adopted a short-term delaying tactic to discourage would-be farmers by purchasing large plots of land, especially in and around Ellsworth.

The problems which beset Abilene and her sister cowtowns were resolved both by economics and force of arms. As for

92: The celebrated Drovers Cottage. Erected by McCoy in Abilene in 1867, part of it was removed by him to Ellsworth where this photograph was made.
COURTESY THE KANSAS STATE HISTORICAL SOCIETY.

the policemen expected to bring about the peaceful subjugation of the 'terrible Texans', they were very much a mixture, few of them real policemen in the Eastern sense. Tom Smith was believed by Henry to have had some training in police methods; but even if this were not true he nevertheless exhibited a control over the Texans which met with general approval. Wild Bill on the other hand had learned his particular skills in the knock-down drag out existence of the early Kansas frontier, the Civil War and the postwar unrest that followed it. Old-timers recalled that he could pulverise a man with his fists if given the chance, but most men who tackled him did so with a gun. Yet for the average cowboy the mere sight of him meandering around in shirt sleeves attached to a 'pair of howitzers' was usually enough to convince most troublemakers that they were out-classed.

For every town marshal who got 'written up' and established a local or national fame, there were as many, equally brave and deserving who never received similar recognition. Like their more famous rivals, few of them were 'professionals' or were in any sense of the word trained for the task. If asked, few would have regarded the job as a vocation, but some by dint of their

93: His parents christened him Bartholomew Masterson; but he preferred to write under his name as William Barclay Masterson and to be known to his friends as plain 'Bat'. As Sheriff of Ford County, Kansas, in 1878-80, he furthered his reputation as a tough customer in a fight or in a chase. Yet Bat hardly ever fired a shot in anger, and only one man is believed to have fallen victim to his pistol.
COURTESY THE KANSAS STATE HISTORICAL SOCIETY.

conscientiousness and dedication created such an impression. It was not even a well paid job. The fabulous sums allegedly paid the 'specialists' such as Hickok, Smith, Masterson and others, would be akin to the reported fortunes paid today to pop stars; but the reality was different. Wild Bill was not paid $1,000 per month to 'clean up' Abilene, but $150 plus a percentage of fines, which even so was high. Smith received the same amount to begin with, but later this was raised to $225 – the highest salary of them all. But such sums were exceptional. Hickok's successor, James B. Gauthie, received only $50 per month, but by then the cattle trade had gone and so had the need for expensive law enforcement.

Other towns regarded the payment of their police as an important issue, and contributions from city coffers were met by additional fines imposed among the gambling, brothel and saloon-keeping fraternity. In Ellsworth the rate for the job as marshal varied according to the season. During the cattle season the marshal received $150 per month, but during the winter this was cut to about half that sum. At one point during a particularly bad time his salary was cut to $100, even during the cattle season; but deputies rarely suffered such setbacks.

They were paid on average $75 a month whether they were permanent or temporary, plus $2.50 for each arrest and a percentage of court fines. Even though the wages of the police force were considerably better than those earned by the cowboy, it was still not a fortune.

To supplement their incomes it was common for cowtown police to resort to gambling themselves, frequently mixing with the very people they were hired to supervise, and if need be to arrest! Among those who indulged in the gambling business on an ownership basis was Wyatt Earp who was employed as a gambler in the Long Branch Saloon and took a percentage of the house 'take'. Later, in Tombstone, he had an 'interest' in the Oriental Saloon and also ran a faro table at the Eagle Brewery Saloon.

The number of policemen who themselves frequented brothels, dance-halls and gambling establishments might have given cause for concern among the city fathers, but it can also be argued that without such a close liaison and watch upon the opposition, few of them would have been so well informed, or able to tackle and eventually tame the Texans on their own terms and in their own environment.

94: Concordia, Kansas, in 1870-1, was not a cowtown, but its rutted streets, false-fronted buildings and frontier style gave it the appearance of one.
COURTESY THE KANSAS STATE HISTORICAL SOCIETY.

5 TRAIL'S END & A NEW BEGINNING

DURING the last six or seven years nearly all the drive has been made up of stock cattle for the ranges north of Texas' wrote W. H. Miller, secretary of the Kansas City Board of Trade in 1884. And he was right, for times were changing fast. The long drives up from Texas to the Kansas markets were slowing down, and other ranges, particularly those in Wyoming, Montana and Colorado, were flourishing.

By the 1880s, the Chisholm Trail, except for the route to Caldwell, was practically closed, and in places part of it was already farmland, a fate shared by many of its rivals. But the Western Trail up to Dodge City and on beyond it to the new ranges was being used to the full. One spot in Kansas made an attempt to resurrect the good old days. It happened in 1885 when, as we shall see, there was much talk about a national trail to the Canadian border, talk in Texas, for northerners no longer wanted Longhorns. The chosen spot, Trail City, astride the Kansas-Colorado line where the national trail would cross the Atchison, Topeka and Santa Fe railroad, began its existence

95: By the end of the trail drives to Kansas there were a number of ranches in the state. Here riders of the Three Block pose in front of their grazing herd.
COURTESY THE KANSAS STATE HISTORICAL SOCIETY.

in 1885 and ended it in 1887, despite the fact that Colorado was a 'wet' state and Kansas – by then – a 'dry' one. The reason for its demise was the failure of the national trail's advocates to sway its critics. The town is remembered now for two good stories, the first being that, as it straddled the state line, a wanted man could escape from a sheriff in either direction with minimum effort. The other story tells how the sporting gals of Trail City would ride over to Coolidge, Kansas, some two miles to the east, advertising their assets in a most effective way: they were stark naked.

More to the point as far as the cattle business was concerned were the important centres like Ogalalla, Cheyenne, Julesburg and Miles City, which were all true cattle towns, and it is estimated that by 1885 a million cattle had been driven up to the northern range that they served. How many survived the harsher conditions is another story.

Barbed wire, which was so to transform the range, dates from the mid-70s. J. F. Glidden, like that other history-maker, Joseph G. McCoy, was an Illinois man, and it was he who took out the first patent for barbed wire – on 24 November 1874. Before the 'Glidden wire' came 'fencing' – on a small scale – which at the time meant walls, hedges etc., and smooth wire, which was by no means cattle proof. The idea of fencing vast tracts had been out of the question because of the cost.

Glidden, anxious to keep his own cows in order, experimented with small spikes at regular intervals on smooth wire and, with I. L. Ellwood, made a machine that would produce the new wire in bulk, but not until a friend of Glidden's named Henry Sanborn joined them did things start happening.

Where cheap fencing was needed was in the West, but the cattlemen were deeply suspicious, fearing damage to their animals with screw worm to follow in the open wounds. A Texas cattleman, Major Andrew Drumm, built a 50 mile long fence in 1876 and a few more followed his example, but most ranchers hated the idea. So Sanborn laid on demonstrations which proved that cattle would avoid the barbs as they normally avoided thorns. The firm was in business, and by 1883 a company using Glidden's patent was producing 600 miles of wire a day.

Moviemakers have made the most of the violence that the wire brought in its train, for settlers protected their spreads with the new wire, then cattlemen did the same to their infinitely vaster spreads, thus provoking their rivals and enemies. We will return to the violence later, merely noting here the enormous amounts of public land that were wired before some government action was taken. One Colorado company wired more than a million acres, and wags were soon suggesting that someone would fence in a whole state. In some areas, postmen had such a job delivering the mail that they started complaining to Washington.

Complaints about sheep – and action against sheepherders

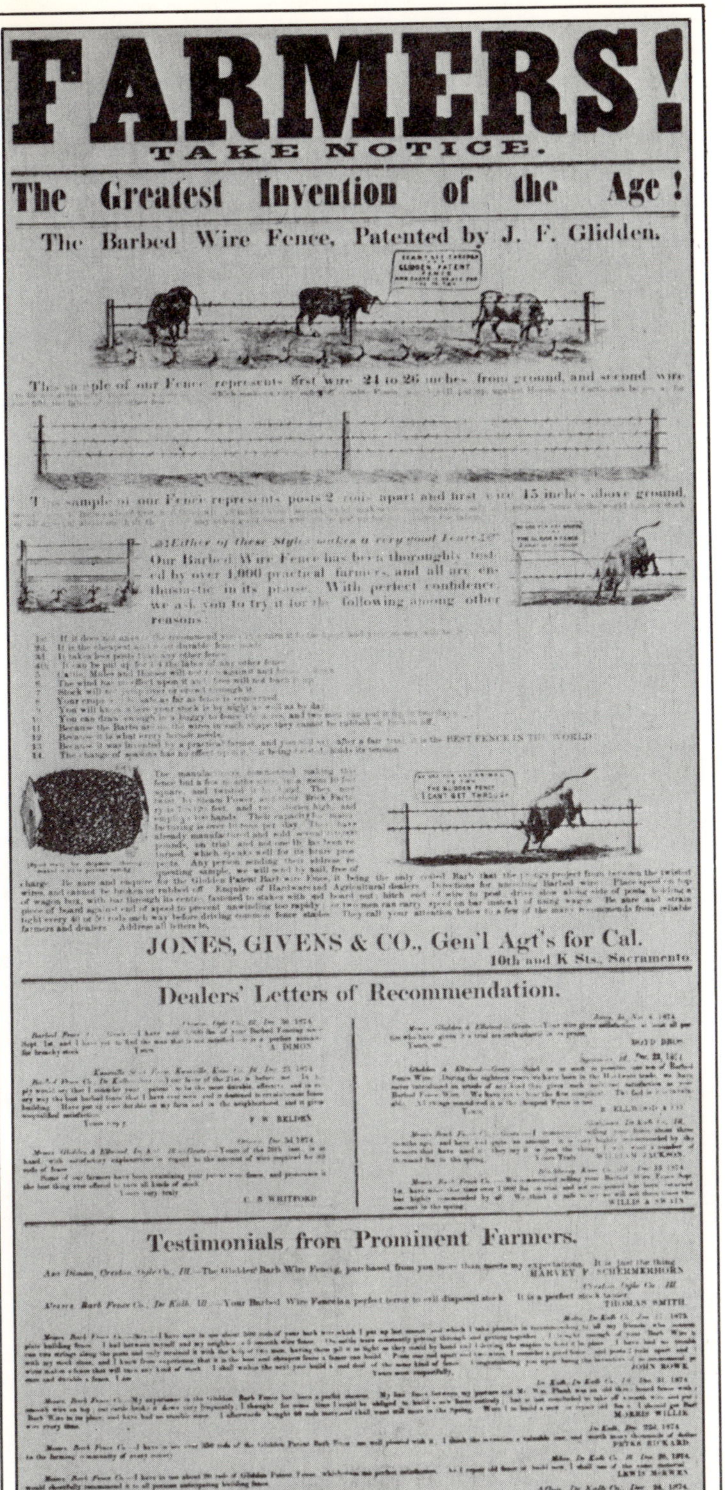

96: Barbed wire – the farmer's friend and the beginning of the end for the cowman's frontier. A typical advertisement of the period.

COURTESY ROBIN MAY COLLECTION.

and their charges – have been exaggerated. The hostility of the average cowboy however has not, though before the 1890s the two groups got along reasonably well and in some cases overlapped.

This has been firmly proved by Robert Howe Woods in *Boscoes, Greasers, and Cowboys? Deflating the Cattlemen vs. Sheepmen Myth*, which appeared in *the Journal of the West*, July 1977. Admittedly, many believed the horror stories of how sheep wrecked a range. But the fact remains that many ranchers went in for sheepfarming as well, including the Marquis de Morès and the huge Swan Land and Cattle Company. Nomadic sheepmen were not popular with cattlemen or sheepmen because they avoided paying local taxes by being constantly on

97: This arrogant-looking cowboy is actually the Marquis de Morès, a Frenchman who became a Cattle King in Dakota Territory until rivals ruined him.
COURTESY THE STATE HISTORICAL SOCIETY OF NORTH DAKOTA.

the move, but the violence came after the end of the open range. This was because grazing lands had become steadily scarcer, and shepherds and sheep died because of it. But sheep, as nearly all cattlemen – and finally their hands – came to realise, were in the West to stay. They had been for many years. By 1885, sheep from the West were producing a third of the national wool-clip, which was the same proportion of production that the cattlemen and their industry had managed by that date. As for the cowboys – 'social misfits who punched cows' as Mr. Woods, generalising rather, calls them – these were the men who could allegedly smell sheep for miles, yet wore jackets lined with wool and put woollen blankets on their horses' backs.

No British authors need fear that they are boasting when relating Britain's involvement in the Western cattle business, for it is Americans who have done most to stress it. That several of the best books about life in the cow country – their titles are mentioned in the bibliography – were written by Britons is gratifying, but what really mattered was the vast amount of money sunk into ranching and, even more significant, the transfer of high-grade cattle from England and Scotland to the West.

Long before the hard-hided Longhorns reached the northern ranges and the Far West, there had been cattle of Anglo-Saxon origin there, the descendants of ones brought across the Atlantic down the years, some of whom had headed westwards along the Oregon and other trails. But there had not been many of them. Longhorn meat was too coarse and stringy for the palates of sophisticated Easterners (immigrants excepted) and was not what Britons expected of imported meat. So a steady stream of purebred and high-grade bulls crossed the ocean, Herefords, above all, because of their exceptional quality. Donald R. Ornduff has some significant information about these in *Aristocrats in the Cattle Country*, which appeared in *The Trail Guide* of The Kansas City Posse of the Westerners in June

98: By the end of the century 'bronco bustin'' was guaranteed to draw large audiences.
COURTESY THE ERWIN E. SMITH COLLECTION OF RANGE LIFE PHOTOGRAPHS, LIBRARY OF CONGRESS.

1964. Refrigeration, which came in the late 1870s, naturally revolutionised the export of beef to Britain, and in the same period the exporting of British bulls began in earnest. 146 head were imported by Alexander Swan of the Swan Land & Cattle Company at Cheyenne. As early as 1878 he was purchasing purebred Hereford bulls in lots of forty at a time. Shorthorns, or Durhams, as they were then called, also appeared, as did Aberdeen and Angus cattle.

The Herefords proved best able to survive the toughest conditions on the range. They reached the edge of the range country not long after the Civil War and cattlemen noted their very heavy rearquarters in contrast to the Longhorns' weakness and cat-hammedness there. They were to become the prime favourite of ranchers in the West and *The Hereford in America*, the history of the breed, proclaimed:

> The inherent stamina, good stout bone and muscle of the Herefords, whose progenitors in England were inured to the yoke, stood them in good stead when they were turned loose on the treeless, windswept American plains. They faced up to the conditions confronting them, not placidly awaiting sustenance but aggressively seeking it wherever it might be found.

Yet neither these Churchillian creatures nor any other breed could be guaranteed to survive the very worst a Western winter could inflict on man and beast. And the worst was the winter of '86-'87.

99: Winter on the range did not stop business, and these drovers are busily engaged in transacting a deal while in the background one man finds time for a shave.
COURTESY ROBIN MAY COLLECTION.

Droughts in Texas, overstocking of the range, and problems caused by the new barbed wire, had done little to lessen the heady euphoria of the early '80s when native and British money was being poured into the industry, but the worst of winters was to alter things so drastically that it would never be the same again. It might be more professional, but the glory days were over.

It was November when the snows started to fall far more deeply than usual, but a warm spell came in early January which allowed the cattlemen and their hands to breathe again. Then on 30 January a blizzard hit the Northwest with an intensity that even the oldest Westerners could not remember having occurred before. Teddy Blue placed the disaster on 3 and 4 February and dubbed it hell without the heat. He told his boss the loss would be ten per cent but within ten days it was seventy five per cent.

An old-timer had instructed him on how to dress for a harsh winter, after warning him that he must dress warmly enough to lie on the prairie if he should break a leg. So his outfit was: two pairs of wool socks, a pair of socks that came up to his knees, moccasins over them, overshoes over the moccasins, two suits of heavy underwear, pants, overalls, chaps and a heavy shirt. He made sleeves out of a woman's stockings, wore wool gloves and mittens, a blanket-lined coat and a big sealskin cap – and he was warm enough 'but not any too warm'.

The following July he saw an old-timer looking up at the sun. 'Where the hell was you last January?'

No one knows how many cattle died that winter, but Teddy Blue's statement that sixty per cent of all the cattle in Montana were dead by 15 March 1887 is a fair estimate of the holocaust.

And those cattlemen who were still in business went back to work . . .

The cattle barons/cattle kings inevitably get most of the attention from historians, but you were a cattleman if you were running the most modest of outfits. Richard Townshend, an Irish-born Englishman whose *A Tenderfoot in Colorado* is one of the most entertaining books ever written about the Old West, was a cattleman without any cowboys for a time. He had come to the West in 1869. Having just survived his first full day there (in Cheyenne), later writing an account of it which is thrilling, informative and amusing in equal parts, he reached Colorado. He and a friend bought some cattle off a Major Oakes:

> They were American cattle, that is to say, the same breed as our English dairy stock, quite unlike the tall, gaunt, long-horned Spanish stock that came from Texas which were now pouring into Southern Colorado. There were about fifty of them and the cows were broke gentle to milk; the head of the herd was old Charley, a big white bull with red ears, the same colour as the wild white cattle of Chillingham, and many of the calves and young stock took their markings from him.

100: Captain Richard King who established an empire in Southern Texas which still exists today as the famous 'King Ranch'.
COURTESY THE DENVER PUBLIC LIBRARY WESTERN HISTORY DEPARTMENT.

While his colleague Lew and Lew's brother Jud were cutting wood to improve the ranch that the trio had planned as their headquarters, Townshend was on his own for days at a time with nothing but his cattle and an unknown number of hostile Indians in the vicinity. Fortunately, they did not appear. Later, starting up on his own, he hired a Texan, Tom Russell, as his only herder. Tom had some cattle of his own, which he ran with a Mexican friend and partner, who worked for a nearby ranch.

> Tom was well-known in the cow-camps and had rather a curious reputation: It was understood that he had killed a man down in Texas in a rough-and tumble fight, killed him justifiably. Tom never posed as a desperado; never did he talk of the killing; but the idea of it was always there and men looked upon him as slightly alarming.

He always satisfied his boss, however, unlike a later Texan (originally from Florida) who thought mavericks were free for killing if beef was short. When the herder suggested killing a stray, Townshend told him that Colorado was not Texas. Explained Townshend: 'There's a cowman's vigilance committee in this county . . . that keeps their little eye open for that sort of thing. I might have to explain my action to a surprise party of masked gentlemen who came provided with a rope.'

Cattlemen great and small had a healthy respect for the masked gentlemen, if they were not already riding with them. The great ones – those that came up from small beginnings – had in many cases done their share of illegal stocking of their own herds, but that did not make them any more tolerant of anyone else. Back East robber barons were making fortunes in a climate of corruption, laissez-faire and piratical late-Victorian business tactics. Few of their Western counterparts were as unsavoury as the worst of them, but they were a high-handed brigade. Many have already appeared in these pages. Among those who have not was George Littlefield, a Southerner, crippled in the Civil War, who succeeded as a cattle baron even though he stated that the only practical knowledge he had gained was 'that a cow will have a calf'. Granville Stuart, Montana's most famous cattleman, who had earlier made the first gold strike in the territory, was the perfect boss for cow-hands, feeding them well, paying them well, helping them if they hit trouble, and even letting them own cattle. Other cattle-men feared that such a policy would lead to branding mavericks and outright stealing, but Stuart – and a handful of others – rightly saw that men who had an interest in the range would be far less likely to rustle.

Some barons were spectacular failures, like the handsome Frenchman, the Marquis de Morès, though he and his wife lived in grandiose style in the Badlands of North Dakota. Others, like Abel (Shanghai) Pierce, were great successes,

101: John Slaughter, Cattle King, and dressed for the part.
COURTESY ARIZONA HISTORICAL SOCIETY LIBRARY.

101.

though few have left more 'quotes' to posterity than the fog-horn-voiced Pierce. His reaction to Glidden's wire was typically colourful, if inaccurate: 'It jest won't do! The cows will jest run into that Glidden wire and cut theirselves. Know what that means? Screw worm! Every open cut means screw worm trouble. It would ruin thousands of head in this country.' While when a neighbour proclaimed the glories of his cow, Pierce bellowed: 'If I had a cow that would give five gallons of milk, I tell you, I'd never touch a teat. I'd make her stick her tongue out, and dip out the milk with a long-handled gourd.' For more about this transplanted Yankee from Rhode Island, who was disappointed not to see any Papal Bulls when he visited the Vatican, consult Chris Emmett's *Shanghai Pierce, A Fair Likeness* (Oklahoma, 1953).

British money poured into the cattleman's West, especially after a Royal Commission on Agriculture sent two Members of Parliament across the Atlantic to examine the industry. They reported back that profit averaged thirty-three per cent and the cash flow was on. By the end of 1882 there were no less than ten big British-American cattle companies. One, the Swan Land and Cattle Company, whose cowboys were paid forty-five dollars a month, was to lose the Scottish investors around half

102: 'Lean, long and lank', a typical cowboy of the early years of this century. No doubt his 'makings' are the famous Gull Durham tobacco brand.
COURTESY PANHANDLE-PLAINS HISTORICAL MUSEUM.

a million dollars, for when the Scots bought the company from Swan, leaving him as manager, Swan started 'misleading' his distant bosses. However, when he went bankrupt – for he had been building up his own empire meanwhile – the Scots made their company prosper once again.

Another Scot, Murdo Mackenzie, managed the Matador Land and Cattle Company like the penny-pinching Caledonian of legend. It had interests in Dakota, Montana and Texas, while the famous XIT ranch was backed by English cash. It was spread over three million acres in the Texas Panhandle and employed up to 150 cowhands at once. Not content with this, the XIT started a second ranch in Montana so that in 1890 general manager Boyce, with a trail linking the two giant spreads, could issue his splendidly simple order to his men: 'Keep your eye on the North Star, and drive straight ahead until you can wet your feet in the waters of the Yellowstone.'

With such vast territorial stakes, it was hardly surprising that the cattle barons could be ruthless if they felt themselves threatened. Not personally, for few of them carried a gun. It was a recognised fact that hands had a way of meting out swift justice on anyone harming their employer, as Billy the Kid remembered just in time when he was pointing a pistol at John

103: Chow time for the cowboys of the Shoe Bar Ranch, from a photograph made circa 1905-10.
COURTESY THE ERWIN E. SMITH COLLECTION OF RANGE LIFE PHOTOGRAPHS, LIBRARY OF CONGRESS.

Chisum and suggesting that he pay up for services rendered during the Lincoln County War.

Property was the name of the game, which made rustling a cardinal offence. Townshend accepted vigilante justice as a fact of Western life but sometimes it was carried out on a vast scale. Of course, it can be argued that instant 'jerking to Jesus' is always wrong, but that argument is almost irrelevant when considering an area totally without law and order or when the law was some days away. Horse stealing was a worse crime than cattle rustling in Western eyes because of the dangers that could befall a man on foot, and cattle thieves could hope to be spared summary justice. A horse thief was extremely fortunate if he escaped hanging.

Of course, many innocent men were executed, of course some died because of private grudges, just as they did in the Reign of Terror in the French Revolution. Of the two most famous Western 'wars' only one of them, the Johnson County War, was strictly a range war, the other, the epic set in Lincoln County, New Mexico, was a power struggle, though many a cowboy and a number of ranchers were involved in it. But before describing the Johnson County episode, that boon to writers and filmmakers, the Vigilantes of Montana must be noted; not the earlier ones described in the book of that name by Thomas Dimsdale, and starring that Napoleon of Western crime, Henry Plummer, but the later variety, masterminded by Granville Stuart, who according to Teddy Blue, 'was the history of Montana'.

Stuart stood no nonsense from anyone red or white, though his ranch with his Shoshone wife and half-Indian children was as real a home as any in the West: Teddy Blue finally managed to get permission to marry one of the daughters named Mary. But 'hostiles' got no sympathy from Stuart. When 1,200 Blackfeet moved from their reservation across the Missouri on to his territory and started running off horses and killing cattle, he did not wait for the military. In the spring of 1881, he entered the Indian camp with some of his men and simply stated that they must pack up their tepees and stay across the Missouri or he would wipe them out. They went.

In 1884 it was the turn of the local white rustlers. Stuart led an expedition against them, leaving behind the young Teddy Roosevelt, then a rancher himself, and the Marquis de Morès, because he didn't want amateurs along. He was serving as the secretary of the Montana Stock Growers Association that year, and there were 429 present at the meeting that declared war on outlawry. Stuart believed in leading from the front, his Winchester .50-95 Express in his hand. Naturally, the controversial campaign that followed created great ill-feeling against Stuart's 'Stranglers' but he never faltered in what he considered his duty, never denied his part in the action, and never told who was with him. When a woman accused him of hanging thirty innocent men, he raised his hat and replied: 'Yes, madam, and by God, I done it alone!'

Even his worst enemies admitted that he – unlike too many vigilantes – was prepared to listen to the evidence before resorting to the rope. He himself related the story of one Billy Downs, suspected of being a horse-thief, cattle-killer and seller of whisky to Indians. As Downs was a family man, he was merely cautioned but, later, vigilantes paid him another visit and ordered him to step outside. Eventually, he appeared with an ill-looking specimen named California Joe, not to be confused with *the* California Joe, Moses Milner, Wild Bill Hickok's friend. Yes, the pair admitted, they had stolen horses from Indians, but never from whites. But their pen contained twenty six horses all with white men's brands on them. They also

104: A roundup on the Sherman Ranch, Genesee County, Kansas, circa 1902.
COURTESY U.S. WAR DEPARTMENT, GENERAL STAFF, NATIONAL ARCHIVES.

claimed that the dried meat in the house was buffalo, though the last buffalo had gone two years before. A newly salted bale of hides had the Fergus Stock Company brand on them. Both men were given 'a suspended sentence'.

Another Granville Stuart story is worth telling, for it indicates the difference between his admittedly ruthless vigilantes and the characters we shall be meeting in the Johnson County War.

Some of Stuart's calves were missing, but near his home ranch he found a rancher 'whose cows invariably had twin calves and frequently triplets, while in that vicinity the range cows', as he related in his *Forty Years on the Frontier*, 'were nearly all barren, and would persist in hanging around this man's corral, envying their numerous children and bawling and lamenting their own childless fate. This state of affairs continued until we were obliged to call around that way and threaten to hang the man if his cows had any more twins.'

Naturally, tales spread how Stuart had settlers killed so as to make more room for his own herds, and no doubt, as noted, private scores were settled by some individuals. But Granville Stuart is known to have helped settlers, notably when he had troubles enough of his own in the terrible winter of '86-'87: we

105: Some of the riders for the Aztec Land and Cattle Company (better known as the Hashknife Outfit) of Holbrook, Arizona Territory in 1887-9, during the Graham/Tewksbury Feud.
COURTESY SMITHSONIAN INSTITUTE.

have Teddy Blue's authority for his actions. And in 1881 he built a schoolhouse for children of his whole district, not just those of ranchers.

In contrast to the drastic but – in the context of Western lawlessness – understandable actions of the Montana Stock Growers Association, the behaviour of the Wyoming Stock Growers Association before and during the Johnson County War was infinitly more unsavoury.

The spiritual home of the WSGA was the plush Cheyenne Club. Owen Wister, author of *The Virginian*, called it 'the pearl of the prairies'. It was said to have the finest steward in America, and visiting Englishmen, used to the delights of club life in Pall Mall or St James's Street, found it very much to their taste as did clubmen from New York, Philadelphia and other sophisticated places back East. 'Anyone for tennis?' was a call that could be heard at the Club a generation or more before it became a stock phrase in Broadway and West End comedies, while what is known of the food sounds considerably better than the average West End club, being the equal of those which catered for gourmets.

Alas, this gentlemen's paradise on the Plains was the scene of a homicidal conspiracy in the early 1890s, but the roots of the trouble went back earlier.

The standard contemporary work on the subject is *The Banditti of the Plains* by A. S. Mercer, which was published in 1894. This savage attack on the infamous cattlemen was said to have been suppressed and even the copies in the Library of Congress stolen, but Charles 'Pat' Hall, writing in the *Annals of Wyoming*, Spring 1977, has discovered that Mercer, though not his book, was a fraud. Apparently a fervent supporter of the small ranchers and settlers of Wyoming, he had actually switched sides, having previously applauded the lynch law practised by the big ranchers. Thus perishes another good story.

But the story he and others told was only too true. Some have defended the actions of the cattle barons, but the most the unbiassed observer can do is understand their motives and actions.

106: This Wyoming cowboy is obviously 'dressed to kill' and enjoying every moment of it. Unlike many of his companions he does not appear to dislike double-action revolvers, for in his holster he is sporting a fine ivory-handled Colt 1878 Model D.A. Army.
COURTESY WYOMING STATE ARCHIVES AND HISTORICAL DEPARTMENT.

106.

As elsewhere, Wyoming's first cattlemen made large or small fortunes on the open range in the 1870s and early '80s, some of them becoming cattle barons. Some, as elsewhere, had climbed to power that much faster by branding strays and rustling – which did not stop them overflowing with righteous rage when later arrivals started doing the same thing. And all the while settlers were arriving in Wyoming and small ranchers starting up business.

Three-quarters of Wyoming's cattle are thought to have perished in the terrible winter which has featured so often in this chapter. After it, Wyoming's cattlemen, like those elsewhere, learnt their lesson, ensured there was hay for winter food and improved their stock but avoided overstocking. But more and more settlers were coming into the beautiful territory, which became a state in 1890. These 'squatters' were an affront to the denizens of the Cheyenne Club and soon cattle barons began regarding all the intruders as rustlers. We will not insult our readers by suggesting that none of them were. Like Montana, Wyoming clearly had its share. But there is no evidence to suggest that the rustlers were in the majority.

The tragedy that followed proved not so much that the cattle barons were corrupt in themselves but that they were corrupted by their power, wealth and ambition into taking lethal action. The WSGA ruled Wyoming politics, which did its members no

107: This Wyoming cowboy favours a single cinch or 'centre-fire' saddle and the stirrup leathers have no jockeys which suggests the saddle is circa the late 1870s or early 1880s.
COURTESY WYOMING STATE ARCHIVES AND HISTORICAL DEPARTMENT.

harm. The governor and its senators were on its roster, so what hope had the small rancher or the granger, as nesters were called in the area, of getting his views across?

The Association excelled itself by passing a 'maverick law', which stipulated that every unbranded calf found on the range should become the property of – the Association. This was said to be an attack on rustlers, but the members sold the strays at auctions where the prices were too steep for small ranchers to buy back their strays.

With the money the cattlemen obtained in this high-handed way, they hired range detectives, who were to receive $250 for convicting a rustler. These cattle detectives were to be found in many parts of the West and the money that was offered them attracted some choice talent. Pat Garrett, slayer of Billy the Kid, was one for a time and another famous 'stock detective' was Tom Horn, who was to be hanged in Wyoming in 1903 for a killing – of a fourteen-year-old – of which many believed him innocent. A decade earlier the Association's chief of detectives was a far less admirable person than the admittedly controversial and boastful Horn. This was Frank Canton, a man whose past included bank robbery, killings, rustling and serving the ordinary people of Johnson County as a lawman – before selling out to the barons. He was later to be a lawman in Oklahoma and in Alaska, and actually lived to be seventy-eight.

108: An alleged photograph of Billy the Kid made about the time he was involved in the Lincoln County War.
COURTESY WESTERN HISTORY COLLECTIONS, UNIVERSITY OF OKLAHOMA LIBRARY.

The beginning of the war happened in 1889 south of Johnson County on the Sweetwater Range, where two homesteaders named Ella Watson and James Averill had settled. Averill ran a store cum saloon and post office and was in no way connected with the cattle business, while his friend Ella, a buxom whore, was said to accept the occasional cow in exchange for her favours, some of the cattle having been rustled.

Unfortunately, the pair were on land claimed by a belligerent, boastful cattle baron named Albert Bothwell. Jim Averill, who was a justice of the peace, had dared to write to the Casper *Weekly Mail* of 7 April and state that cattlemen were speculators and land grabbers. It should be noted that Ella was not guilty of any crime if some of her cattle had been stolen: the cowboys were the guilty ones.

Such an observation is academic in view of what happened. One morning Bothwell and some cronies dragged Jim and Ella from their cabins and strung them up from the same tree without benefit of even a token trial. There was a public outcry at the double lynching so Ella was transformed into 'Cattle Kate' a notorious lady rustler whose execution was 'for the good of the country', as one apologist announced, and the cattle barons seem to have had no doubt about the justice of the proceedings. One member of the Cheyenne Club, Charles Guernsey, who knew Ella and admitted her to be not a bad-looking woman, wrote in *Wyoming Cowboy Days* how Kate and Jim had got off on the wrong foot and ended up by losing all footing whatsoever.

There were no prosecutions then, nor were there any after a homesteader named Waggoner was lynched in June 1891. That November, however, would-be assassins had less luck when they attacked the cabin of W. H. Hall on the Powder River, who happened to be away. Two remained outside while two more broke in. They saw Hall's room-mates, Nathan D. Champion and Ross Gilbertson, lying on their bunks and one of the invaders told them to give up and promptly fired at Champion.

Nate Champion was a Texan of more spirit than anyone in Wyoming then knew. He seized his rifle and drove his assailants out under rapid fire. Though all four fled, two were wounded and left their coats behind, which identified them. The only one arrested left Wyoming on bail.

Next to dic were Orley Jones and John Tisdale, the latter being shot down as he was driving his wagon home with toys for his children. Neither men had ever been accused of rustling. Frank Canton's horse was found near Tisdale's body, which led to his arrest – and release. Feelings in the area against the cattle barons were reaching fever pitch.

The small cattlemen and the grangers now formed themselves into the Northern Wyoming Farmers' and Stock Growers' Association and, meanwhile, the cattle barons were busy preparing an 'extermination' list on which were seventy names. To do the job they decided to hire a gang of gunmen.

109: Cattle Kate (Ella Watson) whose lynching, and similar outrages, were a prelude to the Johnson County Cattle War.
COURTESY DENVER PUBLIC LIBRARY, WESTERN HISTORY DEPARTMENT.

It is this cold-blooded planning which has shocked even those who have tried to study the Johnson County War in what can be termed a neutral manner, which is hard given the known facts. In charge of the avengers was to be portly, pompous Major Frank Wolcott, late of the Union Army, and reasonably competent. Johnson County was to be invaded from without and every telegraph line connecting it to the outside was to be cut. Then the invaders would head for Buffalo, the 'rustlers'' capital, where Sheriff 'Red' Angus and other officials on the side of evil were to be liquidated. Then the genocidal death list could be handled.

Among those interested parties informed in advance of the plan were the Acting Governor, the state senators and senior officials of Union Pacific who provided a killers' special. While horses were being bought outside the state in Colorado to prevent talk, recruiting agents, financed by the WSGA, visited Texas and elsewhere offering gunmen five dollars a day, plus expenses and a bonus for each rustler killed. Employees were to be insured for $3,000. There were plenty of volunteers.

On an April morning in 1892, some fifty-two heavily armed men, almost half of them Texans, climbed down from a Pullman at the Union Pacific depot at Casper, Wyoming. Wolcott's lieutenants were Canton and Luther 'Tom' Smith, never to be confused with Tom Smith of Abilene. Luther Smith was said to have shot seven Negroes in a race riot without lowering his rifle. And there were two newspapermen, both of them – and they can hardly be blamed – believing what they had been told of the situation.

110: Cowboy Erwin Smith with a problem bronco at the O.R. Roundup Camp in 1909.
COURTESY THE ERWIN E. SMITH COLLECTION OF RANGE LIFE PHOTOGRAPHS, LIBRARY OF CONGRESS.

There had already been some trouble in the ranks. The gentlemen stockmen naturally travelled in a different part of the train to the gunmen, and Wolcott was most displeased when Frank Canton dared to visit him. The result was a quarrel which led to the Major's resignation, but when Canton took over as commander he was to prove ineffective and Wolcott gradually regained control.

The invaders of Johnson County headed first for a WSGA member's ranch. There they heard that a band of rustlers was to be found at the KC ranch some fifteen miles on and decided to tackle them before swooping down on Buffalo. The 'band' was to turn out to be Nate Champion and a friend of his, Nick Ray, both of whom were down for extinction. With them were

111: The driving coming in on the Matador Ranch, Texas, from off the Cap Rock, circa 1905.
COURTESY THE ERWIN E. SMITH COLLECTION OF RANGE LIFE PHOTOGRAPHS, LIBRARY OF CONGRESS.

two trappers who had stayed overnight because of a storm.

The cabin was soon surrounded and the trappers emerged one at a time, heading respectively for a creek and a barn, only to be caught, then freed. When they did not return, Nick Ray came out and moments later was crawling back, mortally wounded. Nate rushed out to drag him to safety with one hand, as he fired his six-shooter with the other.

The scene was set for one of the most heroic episodes in Western history. Nate Champion kept his attackers at bay all day long and even managed to leave an account of his fight for his friends. After setting the scene for them, he went on:

> Nick is shot but not dead yet. He is awful sick. I must go and wait on him. It is now about two hours since the first shot. Nick is still alive. They are still shooting and are all around

the house. Boys, there is bullets coming in here like hail. Them fellows is in such shape I can't get at them. They are shooting from the stable and river and back of the house. Nick is dead. He died about 9 o'clock .

Later, Nate saw smoke down at the stable and realised that the invaders had fired it. He confessed to feeling lonesome and wished he had someone else with him so that they could watch all sides at once. Finally, the besiegers propelled a wagon full of hay against the cabin and set fire to it. The last entries in the diary were as follows:

Well, they have just got through shelling the house like hell. I heard them splitting wood. I guess they are going to fire the house tonight. I think I will make a break when night comes, if alive. It's not night yet.
The house is all fired. Goodbye, boys, if I never see you again.

112: The N Bar N cowboys in a relaxed moment during a drive of 300 miles Northwest with 7,000 head in 1890.
COURTESY MONTANA HISTORICAL SOCIETY.

After signing his name, he dashed out of the back door of the cabin, firing his rifle as the first bullet hit him. Twenty-seven more followed, some of them piercing that courageous heart. His killers found his diary and deleted a mention of Canton, then pinned a card on his bloodstained vest – it read 'CATTLE THIEVES BEWARE'.

Sadly, Nate could not know that two men he had earlier seen riding by had eluded their pursuers and – unbeknown to the invaders – had headed for Buffalo. The townspeople were soon up in arms, while Red Angus, finding that neither the National Guard nor the nearest military would help, and failing to get a message to the governor because of the cut wires, rapidly raised a posse and raced towards the invaders.

Morale was somewhat low in the Wolcott camp. Two men badly wounded by Nate had been sent back to Casper, while the rest of the party rode through the night towards Buffalo. Suddenly a messenger appeared to warn them what was going on in town and they retreated to the TA ranch which they had just left. They hastily entrenched themselves, which was just as well, as by mid-day the following morning a swarm of small ranchers and settlers led by Angus had the place surrounded.

On the second day of the siege, and despite every effort of the ordinary people of Johnson County to prevent the wires from being repaired – for it was now to their advantage to defeat the invaders as soon as possible – a message reached Washington, then the President himself. He was told that a state of insurrection existed in Johnson County and – not knowing the truth – ordered troops to rescue the invaders. In the nick of time, after what they thought was their last meal, Wolcott and his men, preparing themselves for a breakout, heard a trumpet and the Major announced: 'Gentlemen, it is the troops!' Minutes later he surrendered, not to 'that man' Red Angus, but to a fellow gentleman, Colonel Horn.

The invaders were taken into what was virtually protective custody and after much legal wrangling the case against them was dropped in January 1893. Criminal charges were brought in the cases of Champion and Ray, but as the two trappers who knew something of what had happened were bribed and sent out of Wyoming, there was no case to answer. The cattle barons felt justified and there was a fine party for all concerned at the Cheyenne Club, but the little men of Wyoming were the true winners and they knew it. Never again could the cattlemen so dominate the range while those on the other side, who had been genuine rustlers, now learned discretion. Finally, cattlemen great and small, and even the grangers, began to co-exist, while Nate Champion deservedly became a hero of almost Homeric proportions. Cowboys even turned his epic diary into song.

113: These Indians are believed to be Caddo or Kickapoos, and were photographed in Woodward County, Oklahoma, about the turn of the century. Some considered the Indian, in particular the Pawnee, as natural herders. Some of them are wearing moccasins instead of conventional boots.

COURTESY WOODWARD COUNTY COLLECTION, WESTERN HISTORY COLLECTIONS, UNIVERSITY OF OKLAHOMA LIBRARY.

114: The Chicago Stockyards circa 1893.
COURTESY ROBIN MAY COLLECTION.

In 1890, two years before the Johnson County War was fought, the Superintendent of the Census in Washington announced that there was no longer a discernible frontier line. The herders had had a last gigantic fling in 1884, driving 300,000 cattle up the trails, but by '87 there were few drives: with the open range dead in the '90s, there were none. Every attempt by vested interests to open a National Trail from the Red River to Canada using the public domain failed. But by then ten million cattle had headed northwards out of Texas, driven by 'social misfits' perhaps, but men of destiny all the same.

There has never been a migration of domestic animals like it in all history. Texas had been saved from poverty and – whatever many Kansans maintained – the Longhorns had helped their state prosper. They changed the nation's favourite meat from pork to beef, though, as we have seen, it was the meat of cattle descended from British stock that was to conquer the national palate, just as those sturdy Herefords, Shorthorns and the rest were to turn the magnificent Longhorns into museum pieces to be bred as pets or for the requirements of Hollywood.

As for the cowboy, he found that homesteaders were human after all and even came to tolerate sheepmen and their sheep, especially when his boss started keeping the woollies himself. 'The farmer and the cowman' were to be urged to be friends in that intoxicating musical, *Oklahoma*, and they finally were. The cowboy's world had been democratic, embracing the most ordinary of men – and aristocrats from the East and from

Britain and Europe as long as they would accept his world and belong to it. But now, in the '90s and beyond they became true democrats, full members of the Western community, as they are to this day.

But they had done something else. After initial, inevitable troubles in the Kansas cowtowns, they had helped heal the wounds of the Civil War, not least because so many of them were to settle in the North – like the heroic Nate Champion. Southerners met Easterners and gradually the two became one. The old-time Texas cowboy vanished into history and myth, but a new figure emerged. Everett Dick has symbolised it when he wrote, 'the southern drawl became the western drawl'.

115: A roundup and branding scene in Arizona Territory in the late 1890s.
COURTESY THE NATIONAL ARCHIVES.

116: A Wyoming cowboy of the 1890s on his home range.
COURTESY WYOMING STATE ARCHIVES AND HISTORICAL DEPARTMENT.

APPENDIX 1

THE CHISHOLM TRAIL & ITS RIVALS

The Chisholm Trail, as we have already noted, was not the only cattle trail for, even before the Civil War, cattle were driven East to New York and as far West as California; but it was by far the most famous. Yet only in recent years have historians established its exact route and clarified the names given to this and other trails, because even the old-timers could not agree among themselves on names and locations! Some even credited the trail to John Chisum, but his activities were confined to New Mexico and the Goodnight-Loving trail.

In the 1920s the late Dr Walter Prescott Webb claimed that the Chisholm Trail was unique 'because there was no such trail – there were trails continually shifting'. Later, in his book *The Great Plains*, he modified this view and said that whether Jesse Chisholm actually laid out the trail was academic, what counted was that the route offered plenty of grass, fordable streams and level terrain – in short, 'a natural highway for cattle'.

117: Gathering hay for feeding on a Nevada ranch.
COURTESY ROBIN MAY COLLECTION.

During the early drives names did not have the importance they do today. To many drovers it was simply 'the trail'; but by 1870 the word 'Chisholm' was in use, and it indicated a specific route. Then, in 1874, the Kansas Pacific Railway in a bid to capture the trade, renamed the route 'The Ellsworth Cattle Trail', and to generate interest in it produced a 'Guide Map of the Great Texas Cattle Trail from Red River Crossing to the Old Reliable Kansas Pacific Railway', which was also republished a year later. An illustrated brochure, it also contained a large folding map of the route and, of great importance, blow-by-blow details of mileage, grazing and watering

118: Cowboys of the CCC Outfit in the early years of this century.
COURTESY THE ARIZONA HISTORICAL SOCIETY LIBRARY.

places on the way. To add to the confusion over names, in 1876 the Department of the Interior's General Land Office published a map depicting the Chisholm Trail as the 'Abilene Trail and Stage Road'.

Part of the problem of identification was because of the other trails also in use, and in the hope of clarifying the situation, the endpaper map was produced to cover the whole period of the drives and includes some of the more important railroad links.

Basically, all the trails had their roots in the Rio Grande region of Texas, but after converging on the Red River they then separated. The early Sedalia, Shawnee and Baxter Springs trails took the more easterly route, while the Goodnight-Loving Trail pushed West and North into Colorado and New Mexico and on up into Wyoming. The Western Trail wound up through Fort Griffin and crossed the Red River at Doan's Store, and up through the Nations (Indian Territory, now Oklahoma) to Dodge City and on to Oglalla. But Chisholm's Trail went due North via Red River Station, up through Indian Territory, and across the Washita, Canadian, North Canadian and Cimarron rivers en route, until it reached present-day Wichita where it officially ended. From then on the trail was known as 'McCoy's Trail' or 'McCoy's Extension', and by some as 'the Abilene

Trail'. For a short period in 1868, cattle were driven on from Abilene to Waterville where they were despatched east on the tracks of the Central Branch of the Union Pacific Railroad. And even Junction City, Russell, Brookville and Hays City (among others) joined in the cattle business, but only briefly.

Early in 1872, when Abilene finally decided to ban the trade, another trail was extended from Wichita to Newton where the Atchison Topeka and Santa Fe Railway had reached the place in August 1871. In May 1872, the Wichita and Southwestern Railroad provided a link to the Santa Fe's main line at Newton, and Wichita took over the trade and kept some of it until 1877. In 1873, at about the point where Caldwell stands, another route was opened up to become 'The Ellsworth Trail', or 'The Texas Cattle Trail'. In 1875, due to increasing settlement, the Ellsworth route was changed and branched off from the Chisholm Trail some miles above Red River Station. Also in 1875 the Western Trail to Dodge City and beyond was established.

Dodge City became the undisputed 'Queen of the Cowtowns' and kept the trade until 1885. But by 1880 she was rivalled by Caldwell, known as 'The Border Queen', which had entered the business very late. Like Wichita she had been on the trail from its early years, but until the arrival of the Cowley, Sumner & Fort Smith Railroad (operated by the Santa Fe) she could not share in the profits of the trade.

As time passed, and civilisation progressed, so the various trails shifted, were obliterated, lost and forgotten. But not the Chisholm Trail. The name has survived in history, legend and song, and even today, if one knows where to look, parts of it can still be seen, weed-strewn and grassless, relics of the once great 600-mile-long highway, sometimes four hundred yards wide and pounded flat and hard by millions of hooves during the greatest mass migration of livestock ever known – surely an epic event that ranks with the great treks of history!

119: Roping a calf on a Wyoming ranch towards the end of the 1890s. The rather magnificent Longhorn against the fence looks on almost disdainfully.
COURTESY WYOMING STATE ARCHIVES AND HISTORICAL DEPARTMENT.

APPENDIX 2

COW COUNTRY WORDS

A check list, elaborating some mentioned in the main text and including others which do not appear elsewhere. For further reading see Western Words *by Ramon Adams (University of Oklahoma Press, 1968).*

ARBUCKLE'S: The cowboy's usual brand of coffee, which the cook was expected to have hot and ready day and night.

BEDROLL: Not simply the cowboy's bedding, but his other equipment rolled up in it. It was waterproof enough to keep a hand dry in heavy rain and, after his horse, boots and saddle, was his most treasured possession, containing his money and valuables. His six-shooter spent much of its time in it.

BOSS HERDER: See TRAIL BOSS.

BRONCO: A wild or half-wild horse, more often known as a bronc (from the Spanish). Thus BRONC BUSTER, a professional horsebreaker, a job so skilful and rugged that few pursued it after the age of thirty.

BUCKER: A horse that pitches. So, BUCKERS, also known as GUT TWISTERS, CLOUD HUNTERS etc and BUCKING.

BUFFALO CHIP: Dried buffalo dung, used as fuel on the Plains, as were COW CHIPS.

BUNKHOUSE: Where cowhands slept on a ranch.

BUSHWACK: To ambush.

CABALLERO: A horseman, particularly a devil-may-care cowboy (from the Spanish for cavalier or knight).

CATTLEMAN: The word is interchangeable with RANCHER and STOCKMAN, the cattleman being a businessman, the capitalist of the range, as opposed to the cowboy, a hired – and often a wandering – hand. There were also the CATTLE KINGS/CATTLE BARONS, many of whom appear in this book. For an entire work devoted to these men, see *The Cattle Kings* by Lewis Atherton (Indiana University Press, 1961).

CAYUSE: Wild Oregon horses, named after the Cayuse Indians. It was first used for western, as opposed to eastern, horses, then for undersized horses; later still, by northern cowboys for any horse.

CHAPARRAL: A thicket of thorny scrubs, cacti, etc (from the Spanish).

CHAPS: Leather leggings used by a cowboy to protect his legs from chaparral, from the weather, from being injured in a fall,

120: Winter range rider by Remington.
COURTESY ROBIN MAY COLLECTION.

etc. The standard ones were 'shotguns', but 'batwings', which could be put on more quickly, became popular, while on the northern ranges 'woolies', with their fronts covered in wool or fur, made for warmth. (From the Spanish, being the shortened form of *chaparejos*, but they are pronounced 'shaps'.)
CHUCK WAGON: The cowboy's mobile kitchen, usually a converted wagon, and run by the legendary autocratic Cookie. Chuck was the cowboy's word for food. As explained in the main text, Charlie Goodnight is regarded as the inventor of the all-important chuck wagon, which contained the hands' bedrolls and was their headquarters away from the ranch.
CINCH: Together with the long leather strap called a *latigo*, it formed a saddle girth. (From the Spanish '*cincha*'.)
CORRAL: An enclosed pen for animals (from the Spanish). A ROPE CORRAL was a temporary one formed by several hands holding ropes to make an obtuse U shape. In it saddle horses were penned until caught for saddling.
COULEE: A dry creek or ravine (from the French).
DOGIE: A motherless calf. Its rather obscure origins rate a long entry in Adams' *Western Words*.
DRAG: The rear of a trail herd, the cattle being the tired, weak, idle, young and dumb. Cowboys riding drag found themselves eating dust for hour after hour, so hands took it in turn to ride drag.
DRAW: A natural drain for rain fall.
DROVER: This was a widely used word in early trail-herding

days, but so forgotten later that it does not appear in *Western Words* and is not explained in most modern books about the cattle trade. Thanks to Everett Dick's masterly *The Long Drive* in the Kansas State Historical Society's *Collections* Volume XVII (1926-28), the authors have been able to explain the drover's job in Chapter Two of this book, notably how it was he who contracted with ranchers in the early days for cattle to drive up the trail, he who selected cowboys and bought a chuck wagon, led the outfit north, and sold the cattle at the end of the trip. It was later that ranchers in growing numbers had their herds driven north by trail bosses, though it must be stressed that some ranchers had driven – or had driven for them – their herds from the beginning. In his *Conquering Our Great American Plains* (1930), Stuart Henry noted different classes of drover. The top class were considerable figures, virtual magnificoes of the trade who stayed at the Drover's Cottage – Henry writes of 'the Drover's Cottage lords' – and who would back up their men when they ran into trouble in a cowtown (one assumes, depending on circumstances). More modest were the drovers who were, in fact, small ranchers, whose wives sometimes joined them in Abilene via the railroad, while there were also a number of drovers who aspired to be magnificoes but were probably refractory cowboys. These would apparently encourage their men in wildness and, unlike the other two groups, they wore six-guns or had them handy.

DRY-GULCH: To ambush or kill.

FORK: The front of a Western saddle, supporting the horn.

GREASER: The cowboy's insulting name for a Mexican.

GRINGO: A contemptuous term in Central and South America for Americans and Britons. It is probably derived from the Spanish *griego*, meaning Greek and in parts of Spain it means all foreigners.

GUT-EATER: One of the names cowboys called Indians, who liked beef entrails.

HACIENDA: A rancher's home (from the Spanish).

HACKAMORE: A halter (from the Spanish word for head-stall).

HAND: A very common cow country word for a cowboy.

HERDER: Though this came to be a name for the sheepherder, it was used to describe cowboys on the trail in the early days.

HOMBRE: A Southwest word for a man, often used in a derogatory sense. (From the Spanish.)

HONDA: The eyelet at the business end of a lariat for making a loop.

HOOLEY-ANN: A roping term, being a rope thrown from the ground or on horseback.

HORN: The saddle's pommel, the last word not being in the cowboy's vocabulary.

HURRICANE DECK: The saddle of a bucking horse.

HYMNS: Songs sung to cattle, including rude ones attached to hymn tunes.

JERKY: Dried meat – buffalo, beef etc. – used by Indians and whites (from the Quechua Indian *charqui*).
JINGLEBOB: An ugly earmark made by a deep slit which left the lower part of the cow's ear flapping down. 'Jinglebob John' Chisum, the New Mexico cattle king, made it famous.
JOHN B: The cowboy hat, named, of course, for John B. Stetson.
JUGHEAD: A stupid horse.
JUSTINS: Cowboy boots. After Joe Justin, maker of fine footwear for the range.
LARIAT: The cowboy's rope (from the Spanish *la reata*). *Vaqueros* made their lariats from braded rawhide, but Americans changed to tough grass, which was cheaper.
LEAD STEER: A steer that was not only tough but a born leader, taking its place at the head of the herd and staying there until the end of the trail. The most famous of them all, Charlie Goodnight's Old Blue, was noted in Chapter 2. Cowboys became very attached to these notably undumb critters.
LEVIS: Cowboy 'overalls' - pants with copper rivets to reinforce pockets and seams. After Levi Strauss.
LICK: The cowboy word for molasses, though also a short form of SALT LICK: where buffalo and cattle licked salt.
LONGHORN: There is so much about the Longhorns in this book that all that needs to be noted here is a fine book about

121: The last drive of the ZIT Cattle Company in 1908, photographed twenty miles north of Glendine, Montana. Ironically, it is horses and not cattle that are taking the trail north.
COURTESY MONTANA HISTORICAL SOCIETY.

them, *The Longhorns* by J. Frank Dobie, who also wrote *A Vaquero of the Brush Country*.
MAVERICK: An unbranded calf, usually of unknown origin and motherless. Named after Colonel Maverick, who is featured in Chapter 1.
MESQUITE: A Southwestern tree or shrub, the plant being covered with thorns. Cattle feed on the fruit if they can find nothing else.
MUSTANG: The wild horse of the West (from the Spanish *mestino*).
NESTER: One of the cowboy's insulting words for a home-

steader. From a distance his spread, with its feed patch encircled by brushwood to protect it from cattle, looked like a huge bird's nest.

NIGHT GUARD: A herd's night watch. Only the cook and the wrangler were exempt.

NIGHTHAWK: In charge of the saddle horses at night, though smaller outfits often did not have one.

ON THE PROD/ON THE PECK: Fighting mad.

OPEN RANGE: Unfenced range.

PAINT: Also known as Pinto (from the Spanish for 'to paint'). A horse with irregular white and colour patterns, which made it popular with Indians and today it has many advocates, but cowboys believed that it was not a good cow horse, being poor in close, quick work. This was a general belief, disputed by many of today's Paint owners.

POINT RIDER/LEAD MAN: One of the men who rode in front of a herd of cattle on the trail. They normally worked in pairs and their job was very responsible and could be dangerous. They were the first to cross rivers and the most likely to be attacked by Indians and outlaws. As the trail boss was often some way ahead, they were the herd's pilots and, working abreast of the leaders and one on each side, they were in charge of changes in direction.

PRAYER BOOK: A cowboy's book of cigarette papers.

RANAHAN/RANNY: A top cowhand.

RANGE BOSS: The man in charge of an outfit run not by an individual but owned by a company back East or in Britain.

RAWHIDE: The very useful hide of a cow or steer from which a number of products were made, including ropes, chair seats, trousers etc, and which was used for patching saddles and many other things. Strips of it bound loose wagon tires. A weak cow was among the word's other Western meanings.

REDEYE: Whisky, which was also called TARANTULA JUICE, TANGLEFOOT, TONSIL VARNISH, BASE BURNER etc.

REMUDA: An outfit's horse herd not under saddle at a particular moment. All were geldings. In the Northwest, the remuda was also called a CAVVY (from the Spanish *caballada*, meaning a band of saddle horses) or a SADDLE BAND.

RODEO: Though now used to describe hugely popular cowboy contests, its true meaning is a cattle roundup (from the Spanish).

ROPE HORSE: A horse trained in the art of roping. A good rope horse has always been essential to a cowboy who hopes to become an expert roper.

SHEEP: Among cowboy insults for 'woollies' were BAA-A-AHS, HOOFED LOCUSTS, MAGGOTS and STINKERS.

SON-OF-A-BITCH STEW: A popular range dish of the sweetbreads, brains and other choice parts of a newly-killed calf. The exact contents varied, but it was regarded as a failure if the hand could tell what was in it. It was said that 'you throw ever'thing in the pot but the hair, horns, and holler'.

TALLY MAN: The man who kept a check on the number of calves branded each roundup.
TENDERFOOT: A newcomer to the range. Originally an imported cow.
TINHORN: A cheap, flashy gambler.
TOP HAND: An expert – or the best – hand in an outfit.
TRAIL BOSS: Also see DROVER: The trail boss was hired by a rancher to drive his herd to market and he was therefore the foreman-commander of the herd, as opposed to the drover in early trailing days who had bought the herd himself from various ranchers. Naturally, the two professions overlapped in period.
VAQUERO: The Southwestern word for a cowboy, especially a Mexican one (from the Spanish).
WAR BAG: A cowboy's bag or sack for his personal belongings – everything from cigarette papers and cartridges to a letter from home.
WOLFER: A man hired to hunt wolves on the range. It was a good, if hazardous, form of out-of-season income.
WRANGLER: The man or boy who herded the saddle horses. It was the most menial job amongst cowboys, but good training for a bright boy. (From the Spanish *caverango*, meaning a person who cares for horses.)

APPENDIX 3

THE COWBOY ON FILM

When Buffalo Bill Cody rescued the cowboy from the ranks of 'the criminal classes' in the 1880s, the Dime Novelists quickly followed, and soon his image as a romantic, nomadic horseman was established in the public's mind. Yet the cowboy has fared far worse on film.

The novelist's cowboy is portrayed as he was – a worker with gunplay of secondary importance. But in many Western films the role is reversed: herding cattle takes second place to shootouts. This was particularly true in the late 1920s, the 1930s and even into the early 1940s, when 'cowboy heroes' became what cynics might be excused for describing as 'Sherlock Holmeses with spurs on'. Gone were the mundane and menial range tasks, rough clothing and workworn boots. Instead they were dressed in immaculate suits, hand-tooled gunbelts, flashy boots, expensive hats, and the trapping on their horses would have cost an old-time cowboy a couple of years' wages.

Such menial tasks as herding cattle were forgotten in favour of frustrating the efforts of crooked land grabbers, or evil men who appeared in a place and announced: 'I now run this town and own everyone in it'. And then there were variations of the same character whose greedy, grasping fingers were in the pie of mining, land speculation, water rights and attempts to wrest some poor rancher or homesteader from his home and property. Against such characters the Western hero, sometimes aided by a comical sidekick or a wonder horse, pitted his wits and his guns to defeat what seemed overwhelming odds. We do not mean for one moment to belittle the heroics of Buck Jones, Tom Mix, Ken Maynard and a host of other beloved heroes of boyhood – far from it! But such antics only serve to show how much the real cowboy has lost out to his 'reel' counterpart.

Perhaps part of the problem lies in the fact that the first film to tell a story was a Western – *The Great Train Robbery*, made in the wilds of New Jersey in 1903. It inspired many imitators and established a tradition: gunfights were in and the scenery, horses and cattle were an essential but secondary part of the whole.

Ironically, by the mid-1890s and at about the time *The Great Train Robbery* was being made, the still camera, which captured the magnificent photographs used in this book, had also inspired pioneer motion picture makers to film cowboys at work and on the trail. Copies of these films are still available and provide a fascinating glimpse into the activities of a breed of men who may or may not have appreciated that they were making history. Yet many years were to pass before the cowboy was to receive anything like the attention on film he deserved.

A glimmer of hope came in the 1920s when several films appeared devoted to aspects of Western life that played an important part in the settlement of the Old West. First came *The Covered Wagon* in 1923, the story of the mass migration across the Plains in the mid-nineteenth century, to be followed by *The Iron Horse* in 1924, the story of the trans-continental railroads; and in 1925 by *The Pony Express*. Later, in 1930, *The Big Trail* added further lustre to the image of the Pioneers, but still the working cowboy was ignored.

Ironically, it was to be 1948 before the cowboy first received cinema recognition when *Red River* directed by Howard Hawks, took audiences by storm. Few but the addicts seemed aware of a cowboy's true purpose, and the sheer spectacle of the trail drive, stampedes and cattle swimming rivers came as a great surprise. Other films followed which placed more emphasis upon the working life of the cowboy, and at long last Hollywood realised that true 'cowboy' films could be popular.

A film in the tradition of *Red River* was *Cowboy*, directed by Delmer Daves and released in 1958, and based upon a fictional episode in Frank Harris's equally fictitious book *On the Trail*. However, *Cowboy* contained one ingredient missing from *Red River*, and that was the dangers faced during transportation of cattle by rail by the 'prodders' and others who accompanied them. These men were constantly patrolling the cars – often roof walking – and had to keep an eye open for cattle that had fallen or were being crushed by stronger companions. A man

122: John Wayne in *Red River*.
COURTESY UNITED ARTISTS.

who entered a rocking freight car full of bawling, frightened and hostile cattle stood little chance if he, too, fell over, or allowed himself to be pinned against the wall of the car.

In the wake of *Cowboy* followed a number of films which dealt with cowboys and cowboy life, perhaps the most notable being the much-acclaimed *Will Penny* in 1967 directed by Will Gries. Similarly, *Monte Walsh*, directed by William Fraker, was about cowboys, in particular their comradeship and loyalty to each other. And no doubt with memories of *Red River* in mind, in 1972 its star, the legendary John Wayne, appeared in *The Cowboys* directed by Mark Rydell. Instead of men to handle his drive he is forced to hire boys, all of whom first have to prove that they can ride and rope as good as a man. Later they avenge his death. *The Culpepper Cattle Company*, directed by Dick Richards, appeared at about the same time and stressed the perils and temptations of the youngsters who wanted to become cowboys.

Even television for a short period did much to popularise the working cowboy. During the late 1950s and early 1960s *Rawhide* thrilled a vast audience; but since then little has been done to perpetuate the real cowboy through this medium.

But if a truly authentic film about cowboys is lacking, the same cannot be said for his cinema image, for at long last audiences are beginning to realise that the cowboy was a special kind of man, and perhaps with time he will become a cinema personality in his own right.

123: Charlton Heston as the ageing cowboy hero of ***Will Penny*****.**
COURTESY PARAMOUNT PICTURES.

APPENDIX 4

THE COWBOY IN FICTION

By 1900 the Dime Novel cowboy enjoyed a wide readership. Small boys avidly followed his adventures and all manner of arduous chores were undertaken uncomplainingly just to earn the money to buy the next exciting episode. But it was not until Owen Wister's *The Virginian* burst upon the scene like a fresh wind blowing across the prairie that the cowboy was taken seriously by adults.

First published in 1902 the book portrays the cowboy as a real person with faults, virtues and a sense of humour. Yet unwittingly, perhaps, by neglecting to give his hero a namc – he is known all through the book only as 'the Virginian' – and by the memorable line 'When you call me that, *smile*!', he created a character that has been with us ever since, the strong silent hero. But the book was concerned more with characters than with cows, and it was 1906 before the real cowboy attracted public attention.

In that year Andy Adams's *The Log of a Cowboy* was published and at once brought into focus the disparity between the fictional cowboy and his historical counterpart. Despite its totally authentic factual origin, it was nonetheless a novel, and like Wister's book was enormously successful. By the 1920s, the fictional cowboy was vying in popularity with the cinema 'Westerns', and novels and 'pulp' Western magazines were read by millions.

Wister has had innumerable imitators and successive rivals, and their names are legion. But perhaps only a few stand out who actually wrote true cowboy stories during their long careers . . . Zane Grey, Ernest Haycox, Max Brand and Luke Short and a handful of others. Among Grey's better known cowboy stories are *The Trail Driver* and *Thirty Thousand on the Hoof.* Other writers while writing of the cowboy have tended to restrict the action not to trail drives, but to range wars, shoot-outs and stampedes all on the home range.

Probably, the image of the cowboy will never change, for the man in the big hat, booted and spurred, and sitting astride his horse silhouetted against the sunset, still evokes a vision of freedom, the wide-open spaces and an independence that has captivated the imaginations of millions.

COWBOY CLASSICS

Before listing some of the principal books on cowboys, the cattle industry and related subjects, tribute must be paid to certain works that the authors have found particularly helpful.

Though a number of articles of exceptional interest have been cited in the main text, one must be mentioned again here, Everett Dick's magnificent *The Long Drive* which is to be found in Volume XVII of the *Collections* of the Kansas State Historical Society (to which we are both proud to belong) for 1926-28. Apart from being a masterly account of its subject and the cattle business as a whole, it was Dr Dick who provided us with a clear exposition of the profession of drover. This was reinforced by a significant section referred to in our text, in *Conquering our Great American Plains* (New York, 1930) by Stuart Henry, who was in Abilene when the Texans arrived.

We Pointed them North by E. C. Abbott (Teddy Blue) and Helena Huntington Smith, apart from its huge entertainment value, has been an inspiration to us and is a veritable mother lode of information about life on the range and the trail, to say nothing of descriptions of bawdy happenings in cowtowns before 'My Reform'. The book is now available in a University of Oklahoma paperback. Perhaps he and his other cowboy/authors were, as William Savage suggests in his superb introduction to *Cowboy Life*, referred to in the introduction of this book, 'little more than men in a state of arrested development' but we dearly wish we could have met him!

Teddy Blue was English born, but R. B. Townshend was an Englishman, Cambridge educated and, later, a member of the Wadham College, Oxford, Common Room. And he was a cowboy and small rancher. His *A Tenderfoot in Colorado* is the best of his three books and is now part of the University of Oklahoma Press's Western Frontier Library. Again it is hugely entertaining and informative – and is also an excellent guide as to how Westerners actually spoke. As for their words, *Western Words* by Ramon Adams, again UOP, is the book to get.

Finally, we owe a debt to Wayne Gard's definitive *The Chisholm Trail* (1954), once more a UOP book and, like his *Frontier Justice*, a standard work as well as an exhilarating one.

ADDITIONAL READING

As well as those described above, the following will be of interest to readers of this book. Only a few have British editions, but many can be obtained by ordering them, while all will eventually reach the reader via the Public Library service.

Adams, Andy, *The Log of a Cowboy* (Lincoln, Nebraska, 1964)

Atherton, Lewis, *The Cattle Kings* (Bloomington, Indiana, 1961)

Bronson, E. B., *Reminiscences of a Ranchman* (Lincoln, 1962, paperback)

Brown, Mark and W. R. Felton, *Before Barbed Wire* (New York, 1956)

Brown, Dee and Martin F. Schmitt, *Trail Driving Days* (New York and London, 1952)

Collinson, Frank, *Life in the Saddle* (Norman, Oklahoma, 1972, paperback)

Cook, James H. *Fifty Years on the Old Frontier* (New Haven, 1923)

Dale, Edward Everett, *The Range Cattle Industry* (Norman, 1969)

Dobie, J. Frank, *The Longhorns* (New York, 1960)

Dykstra, Robert R., *The Cattle Towns* (New York, 1968)

Fletcher, Baylis John, *Up the Trail in '79* (Norman, 1968)

Frantz, Joe B. and Julian Ernest Choate, *The American Cowboy* (Norman, 1955: London, 1956)

Frink, Maurice, W. T. Jackson and Agnes Wright Spring, *When Grass was King* (Colorado, 1956)

Gard, Wayne, *Frontier Justice* (Norman, 1949)

Haley, J. Evetts, *Charles Goodnight: Cowman and Plainsman* (Norman, 1970)

Harris, Charles W., and Buck Rainey (editors), *The Cowboy: Six-Shooters, Songs and Sex* (University of Oklahoma Press, Norman, 1976)

McCoy, Joseph, *Historic Sketches of the Cattle Trails of the West and Southwest* (Kansas City, 1874: facsimile: Columbus, Ohio, Long's College Book Co, 1951)

Mercer, A. S., *The Banditti of the Plains* (Norman, 1968)

Miller, Nyle H. and Joseph W. Snell, *Great Gunfighters of the Kansas Cowtowns* (Lincoln, 1967)

Rollins, Philip Ashton, *The Cowboy* (New York, 1930)

Russell, Don, *The Lives and Legends of Buffalo Bill* (Norman, 1960)

Savage, William W. Jr. ed. *Cowboy Life: Reconstructing an American Myth* (Norman, 1975)

Siringo, Charles A. *A Texas Cowboy or Fifteen Years on the Hurricane Deck of a Spanish Pony* (Lincoln, 1966)

Sonnichsen, C. L., *Cowboys and Cattle Kings: Life on the Range Today* (Norman, 1950)

Stuart, Granville, *Fifty Years on the Frontier* (A. H. Clark, Glendale, 1967)

Webb, Walter Prescott, *The Great Plains* (New York, 1957, paperback)

Wellman, Paul, *The Trampling Herd* (New York, 1951: London, undated/Foulsham)

Westermeier, Clifford P. *Trailing the Cowboy: His Life and Loves as Told by Frontier Journalists* (Caldwell, Idaho, 1955)

INDEX

THE PRINCIPAL TEXAS CATTLE TRAILS

1840 1890

Chisholm Trail
Abilene Trail (McCoy's Extension)
Texas Cattle Trail (Ellsworth Trail) 1874
Texas Cattle Trail (Ellsworth Trail) 1875
Shawnee Trails
Wichita - Newton Extension
Abilene - Waterville Extension
Western Trail
Goodnight - Loving Trail
Sedalia Trail